P9-DVV-149

TOURING IN WINE COUNTRY

THE RHONE

MITCHELL BEAZLEY

TOURING IN WINE COUNTRY
THE RHONE

HUBRECHT DUIJKER

SERIES EDITOR
HUGH JOHNSON

Contents

Touring in Wine Country
The Rhône
By Hubrecht Duijker

First published in Great Britain in 1998 by Mitchell Beazley, an imprint of Reed Consumer Books Limited, 25 Victoria Street, London SW1H 0EX and Auckland and Melbourne

Copyright © Reed Consumer Books Limited 1998
Text copyright © Hubrecht Duijker 1998
Map copyrights © Reed Consumer Books Limited 1998

All rights reserved. No part of this book may be reproduced, stored in a database or retrieval system, or published in any form or in any way, electronically, mechanically, by print, photoprint, microfilm or any other means without prior written permission from the publisher.

Although all reasonable care has been taken during the preparation of this edition, the publisher, editor and author cannot accept responsibility for any consequences arising from its use or from the information it contains.

ISBN 1 84000 047 3

A CIP catalogue record for this book is available from the British Library

Commissioning Editor: Sue Jamieson
Executive Art Editor: Fiona Knowles
Project Editor: Jamie Ambrose
Senior Art Editor: Wayne Blades
Picture Research: Claire Gouldstone
Index/Gazetteer: Ann Barrett
Design: Watermark Communications
Production: Rachel Lynch
Cartographic Editor: Zoë Goodwin
Cartography: Map Creation Limited

Typeset in Bembo and Gill Sans
Printed and bound by Toppan Printing Company Limited, Hong Kong

The Southern Rhône   108

Glossary   144

Gazetteer   146

Index   148

Maps

Foreword

Hubrecht Duijker clocks up the mileage of a road haulier in his peregrinations back and forth across the wine countries of Europe. If anyone knows France (viticultural France, at least) like the back of his hand, it is Hubrecht.

With his first ground-breaking book on the less-famous chateaux of Bordeaux, he invented a genre: the personal, in-depth investigation of wine-growers, their wines, families, homes and tastes – all illustrated with his excellent photographs. In our *Wine Touring Guides*, he reorganises his thoughts and experiences to lead wine-tourists on the routes he knows so well: to his favourite producers, favourite hotels and restaurants, and to the sights, landscapes, markets and monuments that give the visitor the truest feel of each region.

The Rhône Valley has made more ripples in the past decade than any other French region. Suddenly, the penny seems to have dropped; the Rhône's own grape varieties have worldwide application. Syrah (masquerading as Shiraz) has been the backbone of Australian reds for a century, but it is only now that the exceptional character of Rhône wines – red and white – is becoming common knowledge. As the principal north-south corridor of France, the most direct link between northern Europe and the Mediterranean, the Rhône Valley is packed with history. As a thronging land-route (barge-route, too), it is also packed with industry and commerce. Yet the vineyards of the northern Rhône remain tucked away on inaccessible hillsides, corners of deep country in an increasingly urban environment. There is nowhere for them to expand.

Further south, where the valley widens towards the sea, the conditions in its old flood-plain are completely different. The broad, stony fields of Châteauneuf-du-Pape and the villages of the Côtes du Rhône are a world apart from the steep terraces of Côte-Rôtie. Here we are in the ancient Roman *provinicia*, amid some of the finest survivals of architecture and engineering of a civilization that can make our own look puny. In such a public place with so much history, one might expect that everything worth knowing has already been exploited. But it is one of the mysteries and still-unfolding delights of the Rhône that this is not so. Surprisingly, there are appellations such as Cornas and St-Joseph, as well as several of the up-and-coming villages of the Côtes du Rhône, that few outside the region are aware of – certainly that their own producers are just beginning to, as the French say, *mettre en valeur*.

Touring in wine country, calling on producers, visiting their markets and restaurants and picnicking among their vines can be one of the most rewarding of all forms of travel. What other experience, after all, can you carry back home, bottled, to drink at your leisure?

Hugh Johnson

Introduction

Mention the word 'Rhône' and most people think of two things: a river and wine. As it happens, the two are inextricably linked, for wine has been produced in the Rhône Valley for centuries – probably earlier, in fact, than in any other area of France. It should come as no surprise, then, that the Rhône has become one of France's most important wine regions. As such, it makes an ideal destination for the wine tourist.

Following the course of the River Rhône and its tributaries, the Rhône wine region covers almost the entire valley that stretches from Vienne in the north to Avignon in the south. It offers an astonishing array of landscapes: there are steep slopes and jagged mountains, undulating fields, gentle hills and sweeping plateaux.

As might be expected, one of the oldest wine regions is also steeped in history. For centuries, the river has brought diverse peoples into this part of France. As a strategic north-south corridor, the Rhône Valley was often a cause of conflict, a fact which led to the construction of numerous castles and other fortifications, not to mention the courts of the seven popes of Avignon. The remnants of all these influences make the area a huge, open-air museum – a storehouse of archaeological finds and a rich variety of architectural styles which trace the development of the various races and kingdoms that, at one time or another, called the Rhône Valley home.

One thing all these different cultures had in common, however, was a love of wine, as testified by the vineyards that continue to flourish throughout the entire region. In Côte-Rôtie, Condrieu and Cornas, for example, the vines frequently grow up steep hillsides on narrow terraces, while those in Hermitage climb the hill's mainly granite slopes. Vineyards in Châteauneuf-du-Pape often flourish on flat

Left *Château Grillet, near Condrieu, where a high mica content in the soil yields highly individual Viognier.*

Above *The steep, almost vertical slopes of Côte-Rôtie tax the energies of even the most dedicated vignerons.*

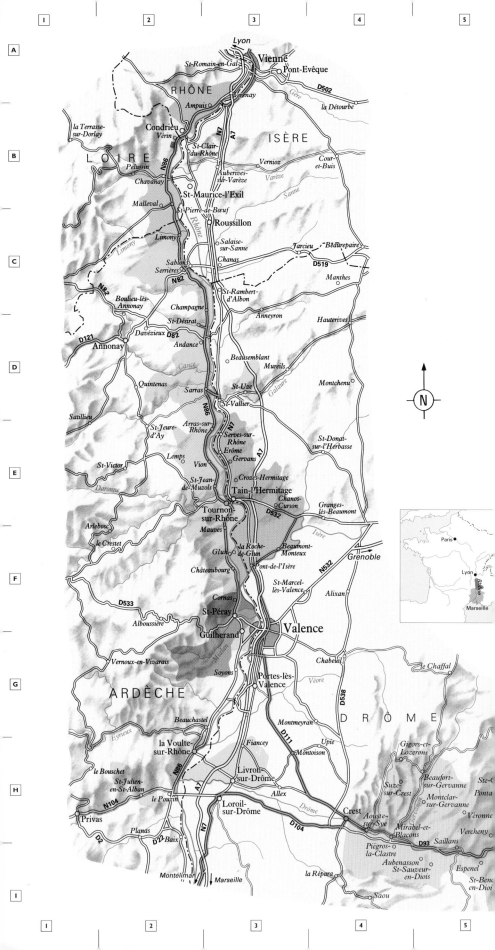

plateaux strewn with stones which store and reflect the heat of the sun. The result of such contrasts is a varied assortment of wines; thus, anyone travelling through the Rhône Valley is going on a wine-tasting adventure.

THE RIVER

The river which gives its name to the Rhône region begins its journey in Switzerland, where it is fed by dozens of glaciers, filling Lake Geneva before continuing on its course. Not far downstream, it enters France and makes it way to Lyon, from whence it flows almost due south until it reaches the Mediterranean.

The Rhône is one of France's most important rivers, not only because of its size, but because of its power. Known traditionally as the 'wild Rhône', it has all too often overflowed its banks, wrecked bridges and boats, left towns and villages under water, and brought death and destruction to all it touched. Here and there are reminders of the damage it caused in the past: of the original 19 arches of the famous bridge at Avignon, for example, 15 have been swept away by floods over the years.

Today, the course of the Rhône has been brought under control by a network of canals and other vast engineering schemes. But despite the intervention of man, it remains a mighty river, flowing majestically through the landscape. The volume of water increases as it flows south, swollen by a number of important tributaries. The River Saône joins the Rhône at Lyon, the Isère meets it at Valence, followed by the Drôme a little further south. The Ardèche merges with it at Pont-St-Esprit, the Durance just below Avignon.

Before the coming of modern transport, rivers were the main traffic arteries in many places, and this was certainly true of the Rhône. Until the advent of the railroad, fruits and vegetables from the south were loaded onto barges at Avignon and pulled northwards on the river by horses as far as Lyon and beyond. Early travellers, too, made use of the Rhône, sailing southwards on its swift currents – a journey which, in those days, took steady nerves and no little amount of navigation skills to complete. Nowadays, though, both people and produce travel either by rail or by *autoroute*, but the river is still in thrall to industry: its fast-flowing current generates electricity and cools nuclear power stations.

The Rhône and the Drôme Valley

– · – · –	Département boundary
	Côte Rôtie
	Château Grillet
	Condrieu
	Condrieu/St-Joseph
	St-Joseph
	Hermitage
	Crozes-Hermitage
	Cornas
	St-Péray
	Côtes du Rhône
	Die
	Wine route

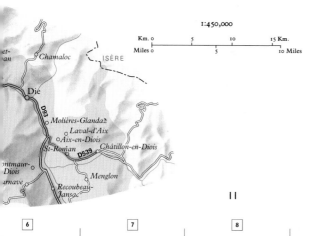

1:450,000

Km. 0   5   10   15 Km.
Miles 0   5   10 Miles

CLIMATE

The rich and varied landscape of the Rhône Valley is complemented by the great range of plants – fruits, vegetables, flowers and herbs – that grow within it. The flora of the Vaucluse, the wide plateau south of Mont Ventoux, comprises 1,800 different species alone. Supporting this wealth of plant life is a climate that is mild throughout the entire valley – with a few variations, of course. Temperatures are higher in the south, which has a more Mediterranean feel, than in the north, which is decidedly more Continental. Avignon, for example, has an annual mean temperature of about 13.5°C, while Vienne's is 11.5°C. There are also significant differences in rainfall: the annual averages for these two towns are 650 and 810 millimetres, respectively.

Another factor that greatly influences the Rhône's weather is the *mistral*, a strong wind that makes itself felt for up to 130 days a year, particularly in autumn and winter.

The name comes from the adjective *maestral*, meaning 'masterful', and once experienced, it is easy to understand just how apt a name it is. The *mistral* always blows from an area of high pressure to one of low pressure – in this case, from the Massif Central, the wide plateau rising west of the Rhône/Saône Valley, to the Mediterranean. It usually lowers the temperature by around ten degrees, and its power is tremendous: it can easily reach speeds of 100 kilometres an hour, and it has been clocked at 250 kilometres an hour on the summit of Mont Ventoux.

Because of the *mistral*'s powerful lashing, dark rows of cypress trees have been planted all over the southern part of the Rhône Valley to protect both its inhabitants and its vegetation from the full force of the wind. Since the *mistral* frequently blows for three, six or even nine days at a stretch, it is not unusual for the people exposed to its buffeting to become depressed and irritable. Despite its unpleasantness, though, the *mistral* does have some beneficial effects – particularly as far as grapevines are concerned. The wind keeps the vines dry, which helps protect them from pests and fungal diseases, and around harvest time, a strong *mistral* has the added bonus of concentrating juice and extract in the grapes as well as increasing sugar levels.

The many faces of the Rhône. Just as climate varies dramatically from north to south, so too does the landscape – and with it, the wines. In the north, Syrah vines flourish on the formidable, steep slopes around Ampuis (far left), while the galets of Châteauneuf-du-Pape (above) mean that the flatter southern Rhône is perfect for Grenache. Meanwhile, in the southeastern Rhône, some vineyards of the Vaucluse département (left) benefit from the shelter provided by the Dentelles de Montmirail. In appellations such as Gigondas, Grenache is also one of the major grape varieties planted.

The Rhône Valley
in history

The Rhône Valley was inhabited as far back as the Stone Age, as is clear from prehistoric finds. In the Bronze Age, the Ligurians, a primitive people thought to have originated in Africa, were using the river as a waterway. They were followed by Celtic tribes such as the Allobroges, who settled in the valley around 600BC. At roughly the same time, a wave of Greek immigrants from the city of Phocaea entered southern France and eventually migrated northwards; archaeologists believe these people were responsible for bringing vines into the Rhône region, which they planted far up into the valley. In any case, Greek amphorae have been found at the town of Tain-l'Hermitage, which lies at the foot of the hill of Hermitage, and wine has been a vital part of the Rhône's history ever since.

THE ROMAN INHERITANCE
After a campaign which took them through the Rhône Valley, the Romans succeeded in defeating the Allobroges at Bollène in 121BC. That same year, they established themselves at Vienne, which subsequently grew into an important Roman

town, the capital of central Gaul. Vienne wine – probably from the slopes that produce today's Côte-Rôtie – acquired a good reputation in Rome, where it became known as *vinum picatum*: wine stabilised with pitch to enable it to travel. While modern palates would probably find this piney flavour a bit hard to swallow, it was popular among the Romans, and Pliny the Elder (among others) commended it highly.

The Romans were to remain in Gaul for over four centuries, and during that time, winegrowing developed strongly in the Rhône Valley and elsewhere. However, the occupying powers did not pursue viticulture simply to quench Roman thirsts. Grape growing was also practised for security reasons: Julius Caesar had riverbanks and nearby slopes cleared of their vegetation and planted with vineyards to make it more difficult for enemies to lay ambushes – a procedure that did not decline until the first century AD. By that time, the Roman empire had too much wine and too little grain, so the emperor Domitian ordered many Gallic vineyards uprooted, particularly in Provence. Yet the trend did not last: in 210AD, the ruler Probus reversed Domitian's edict, and the vines were replanted.

Images of Bacchus, pitchers, presses and other wine-related objects which provide proof of this Roman love affair with wine have been found throughout the Rhône Valley. In the north of the region, terraces created by the Romans for planting vines are still in use today.

Grapes may have been brought into France by other nationalities, but as the Roman empire spread and built impressive cities such as that at Vaison-la-Romaine (below, left), it also established vineyards alongside them. These continued to be cultivated once medieval châteaux (below, right) had replaced the temples – proving, as modern vignerons (left) maintain, that wine is an essential part of any civilised society.

THE ARRIVAL OF THE POPES

From the fourth century onwards, the Rhône was forced to endure wave after wave of barbaric invasions, culminating in 732AD, when the Frank, Charles Martel, defeated the Moors in the bloody Battle of Tours. Winegrowing fell into decline, and it was not revived in any measure until the ninth century, when Christian monasteries began to re-establish some of the vineyards. Yet despite the unifying influence of the church, the Middle Ages proved to be just as difficult a time for the people of the Rhône as the age of invasions that preceded it. There was a great deal of warfare, and feudal overlords fortified their villages with defensive walls and castles.

However, the arrival of the Catholic popes in Avignon provided a powerful economic boost for the surrounding area. The first of the Avignon popes was Clement V, born in Bordeaux, who was installed in Avignon in 1309. The decision to move the Holy See to Avignon was mainly a political one: the French king, Philip the Fair, had several quarrels with Rome, and it suited him to have the Holy Father within his sphere of influence. Yet Clement V did not adjust very well to Avignon; eventually he moved the papal court to Carpentras. His predecessors, however, returned to Avignon and remained there until 1377, and the presence of the popes benefited the Rhône region's economy, as well as affording it a degree of protection. A great deal of building was carried out during this period, and visitors thronged to Avignon and its outlying towns. Of course, they and the papal court all had to be supplied with food and wine.

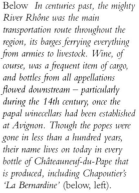

Below *In centuries past, the mighty River Rhône was the main transportation route throughout the region, its barges ferrying everything from armies to livestock. Wine, of course, was a frequent item of cargo, and bottles from all appellations flowed downstream – particularly during the 14th century, once the papal winecellars had been established at Avignon. Though the popes were gone in less than a hundred years, their name lives on today in every bottle of Châteauneuf-du-Pape that is produced, including Chapoutier's 'La Bernardine' (below, left).*

RELIGIOUS AND OTHER WARS

During the 15th century, the Rhône came largely under the rule of the French kings, a reign which brought with it a longed-for stability. In the north, the city of Lyon developed into a centre of international trade – particularly in silk – bringing increasing traffic to the river. In the mid-16th century, however, the area became embroiled in the Protestant/Catholic Wars of Religion, and its new-found prosperity suffered severely as a result. Many churches and other religious monuments were plundered, laid waste or burned. The French Revolution of the 1700s also left its mark on towns such as Bédoin, situated in the Côtes du Ventoux, where a monument commemorates the execution of dozens of villagers.

And the battles did not stop there. During the Second World War, fierce fighting occurred at various locations, including Montélimar, and the castle at Châteauneuf-du-Pape was blown up by the German army. But today, such conflict is just a memory, and the now-peaceful valley has much beauty to offer any who come to explore it.

Viticulture and wines

According to archaeological evidence, the first vines were planted in the Rhône Valley about 2,500 years ago, most probably on the dramatic hill of Hermitage, east of Tournon. Syrah could well have been one of the earliest grape varieties to grow here, for the grape is still abundant in the area.

Despite its long viticultural history, and the presence of some familiar and renowned wines, the Rhône became significant as a wine region only in the latter part of the 20th century. Important factors in this growth include the decline of the silkworm industry in the mid-19th century (which freed land for the planting of vines as opposed to mulberry bushes) and the arrival of the tractor, which made it possible to work the land more efficiently. In 1950, there were some 16,000 hectares of vineyards; today, that figure is 75,000 to 80,000. This phenomenal growth in area was further accentuated by a rise in the yield per hectare.

Better methods of cultivation and stronger vines have further increased these yields – particularly for the Côtes du Rhône appellation, which by itself accounts for 60 per cent of all the wine produced in the entire Rhône Valley. As for the Rhône region as a whole, today it ranks as the third-largest producer in France, after Bordeaux and the Languedoc.

Coopératives – usually *caves coopératives* in French – play a key role in Rhône winemaking; about 70 are active throughout the valley. In the southern Rhône Valley in particular, which supplies the bulk of the region's wine, the lion's share of the vintage is vinified by the cooperatives.

But there is much more to be tasted here than basic Côtes du Rhône. In its cellars and restaurants, visitors to the Rhône will experience just how broad the present spectrum of wines is. For a start, there are various types of sparkling wine, a growing number of dry whites, many different reds (ranging in price from dirt-cheap to astronomically expensive), quite a few rosés, and – just to round off the selection – some dessert wines.

CLASSIFICATION

Most of the present *appellations contrôlées,* or ACs, within the Rhône region date from the 20th century. Only occasionally do mentions of Rhône wines by name turn up in old manuscripts. One of these is Tavel, the celebrated rosé. In the 13th century, King Philip the Fair drank it and praised it – just as other members of the nobility did in later years. Similarly, Cornas was first mentioned by name during the 14th century, but it was not until 400 years later that the first locally bottled Châteauneuf-du-Pape appeared from Château la Nerthe.

The first move towards a protective set of laws for wine came from the town of Roquemaure, which, around 1750, was ranked as the most important wine centre in

Top Vines have flourished in the Rhône for centuries on all types of terrain, yet winegrowing became a significant force only in the late-1900s.

Above *The La Chapelle vineyard on the hill of Hermitage. It is likely that the first vines in the Rhône were planted here around 2,500 years ago.*

the whole of the valley. Here the decision was taken to transport the wine from particular communities in casks which had the letters *CdR* burned upon them – an abbreviation for Côtes du Rhône. This practice was maintained until the beginning of the 20th century, and turned the words 'Côtes du Rhône' into a concept.

A more detailed quality protection came in 1923 from Baron Pierre Le Roy de Boiseaumarie, the owner of Château Fortia, one of the most important estates in Châteauneuf-du-Pape. He led an association of *vignerons* which drafted rules containing detailed production stipulations, and these became the model for the 1936 legislation on ACs for the whole of France. Naturally, Châteauneuf-du-Pape was one of the first wines to be recognised under the new laws. Baron Le Roy was appointed chairman of the executive body concerned, and his name lives on in a number of winegrowing communities. One such is the village of St-Laurent-des-Arbres, where a long street is named after him.

WINE STYLES

Alongside the basic Côtes du Rhône *appellation contrôlée*, which is principally red, there are a number of related wine ACs in the Rhône region. For example, there are Côtes du

Ventoux and Coteaux du Tricastin wines, and a variant with rather more strength, class and concentration, Côtes du Rhône-Villages. This particular wine comes from a few dozen selected *communes*, the 16 most important of which are allowed to have their village names printed on the labels.

All these wines are usually made from various grape varieties, Grenache being chief among them. Since the 1970s and '80s, the average quality has become far more reliable as both cooperatives and private producers have invested in better cellar equipment. In addition, wine-growers are being trained to higher standards. At the same time, the character of Côtes du Rhône and its kindred wines has become less homogenous. There are traditional, powerful wines with a firm, warming taste and a spicy aroma, and then there are very supple, fruity wines strongly reminiscent of Beaujolais. Because of the interest in Beaujolais – and its expensiveness – quite a few Côtes du Rhône producers are evidently seeing their wine as a possible substitute in a lower price band.

In parallel with the reds, Côtes du Rhône white wines have also become more attractive, but they have yet to be fully accepted by a wary public.

Above *A grower samples some St-Joseph, but the wine in his glass will taste like no other in the same AC. Vineyards in this appellation vary enormously – which is precisely why there is no such thing as a 'typical' Rhône wine.*
Right *Across the river, grapes are harvested in Tain-l'Hermitage. Vineyards such as this can yield everything from powerful Hermitage to basic Côtes du Rhône.*

INCREASES IN QUALITY AND PRICE

Improvements have not been confined to basic Côtes du Rhône wines alone. In recent decades, the quality of wines from smaller, individual *appellations contrôlées* has also risen significantly. In a number of cases this has led to a great increase in interest, with very high prices as a result. Until the Second World War, for instance, Côte-Rôtie was served in the region's cafés and restaurants as a simple table wine. It was not until the 1960s that it began to acquire a reputation, but even then it still had to be sold at cost price. The real international breakthrough for this particular wine did not come about until the 1980s, and the best are now as costly as the great wines of Burgundy or Bordeaux. The same is true for red and white Hermitage.

Other Rhône wine prices – including those for Cornas and the better Châteauneuf-du-Papes – have been towed along in the wake of these giants. In price alone there is now a great contrast between the bulk wines that are obtainable everywhere and the much rarer, top-quality wines.

There are also contrasts among wines from different appellations. For example, most wines from the north and the centre of the valley are made from a single grape variety (Syrah), although a small percentage of one other variety might be allowed in a blend. In the south, on the other hand, a number of varieties are generally used: red Châteauneuf-du-Pape is allowed to contain up to 13 grape varieties. Examples of southern red wines from a single grape variety are Côte-Rôtie red (which may also contain some white Viognier), Hermitage, Crozes-Hermitage, St-Joseph and Cornas; white single-variety wines include Condrieu and Château Grillet.

There are also contrasts in the vineyards themselves, due in part to the climatic differences between the northern and southern areas. You can taste worlds of difference throughout the region, starting with a gently sparkling Clairette de Die, then moving on to a generous, white Châteauneuf-du-Pape, a fiery, red Gigondas, a juicy Tavel rosé, and finally to a luxuriously sweet Muscat de Beaumes-de-Venise. The wines offered in this valley are as rich and varied as its landscape.

Rhône grape varieties

The names of grape varieties sometimes appear in this guide when wines are being described, and such references will occur more frequently among the wine producers you meet in the valley itself. What follows is a survey of the most prevalent grapes used to make wine in the Rhône Valley.

RED VARIETIES
Grenache
A grape with plenty of sugar, and therefore plenty of alcohol. Grenache is the base grape used in red *vins de pays*, as well as in Gigondas, Vacqueyras and Tavel rosé. It occurs only rarely in the northern and central parts of the Rhône Valley, due to its sensitivity to cooler temperatures. Grenache needs eight days of fine weather when it is in flower; otherwise, irregularities occur in the setting of its fruit. Wine made from Grenache gains in quality when lighter and more aromatic wines from other grapes (such as Syrah, Cinsaut or Mourvèdre) are added in the blend.

Syrah
The variety with the greatest potential for quality in the Rhône wine region. Superior wines are made from Syrah on its own, or from a blend in which a considerable percentage of Syrah is present. This grape yields aromatic, firm wine that is rich in colour and contains berry-like fruit

Left Not the most prevalent grape in the Rhône by any means, Cinsaut is still important as a 'lightener' for heavier wines.

and good tannin. The Syrah vine can be recognised by the slightly dusty underside of its leaves. It is predominant in the north and centre of the Rhône Valley, where it is usually the only red grape to be grown or used.

Cinsaut (or Cinsault)
A very productive grape, yielding elegant, supple, fruity wines that are not too high in alcohol and not so dark in colour as some. Cinsaut adds elegance to heavier blends.

Mourvèdre
Wine made from Mourvèdre has plenty of colour and tannin, so it is often used to give some backbone to lighter, perhaps over-supple blends. Not suitable for all types of soil, this grape ripens comparatively late and is not high-yielding.

Carignan
Carignan is a relatively simple grape from which pleasant, fruity wines can be made by using special fermentation methods such as *macération carbonique* (carbonic maceration), in which the grapes undergo a second fermentation in the presence of carbon dioxide.

WHITE VARIETIES
Clairette
Clairette is a grape that likes the sun and gives best results in poor soil. Thanks to modern winemaking techniques, fresh-tasting wines can now be made from it, and also sparkling wines – particularly around the town of Die in the Drôme Valley.

Roussanne
Roussanne yields wines with good fruit and a certain breeding. Its vine leaf shows some similarities to that of Syrah, but it is fairly susceptible to plant diseases.

Marsanne
Often used in combination with Roussanne, Marsanne yields a wine with a somewhat fuller taste, but less finesse. The vine is quite disease-resistant.

Viognier
An exceptionally sensitive grape; however, plantings of it are increasing, both in Condrieu – where it is the only variety – and further south in the valley in the Côtes du Rhône and Côtes du Rhône-Villages areas. Viognier yields fragrant, delicate, fresh wines with a firm core and a good deal of charm.

Muscat
This grape is made into sparkling wine (in the Drôme Valley) and, with some additional alcohol, into the sweet dessert wine known as Muscat de Beaumes-de-Venise. The resulting wine has the aroma of freshly picked grapes.

Above Though difficult to grow, Viognier is gaining popularity. Planting is on the increase, due to the fine, aromatic white wines it produces.

The cuisine

Throughout the Rhône Valley, even in the smallest villages, local markets are characterised by a super-abundance of fruit and vegetables. Naturally these fresh ingredients are used copiously in the region's restaurants, and large quantities are sent to Paris or abroad.

Among the fruits that flourish here are melons; in fact, the Rhône Valley is the main supplier of melons, apples, cherries and dessert grapes to the whole of France. Its fertile soil also yields pears, plums, nectarines, peaches, raspberries and blackcurrants. The most commonly grown vegetables include tomatoes, courgettes, onions, asparagus, lettuces, artichokes, aubergines and garlic. Almonds and walnuts are also cultivated, as are olives – the town of Nyons is famed for its black and green olives, and it holds olive festivals a couple of times a year.

Above Not for nothing is the town of Nyons known as the ' olive capital'. Both black and green varieties abound here and in other parts of the southern Rhône. Left Even in the tiniest village, fruit and vegetable markets are a delight, offering a fascinatingly wide range of produce which, fortunately, finds its way into the kitchens of local restaurants.

The southern part of the Rhône Valley belongs to Provence, and so the characteristic herbs of that region may be found in abundance. With the Mediterranean close by, the Rhône also has an ample supply of fresh seafood. The upland rivers and streams provide freshwater fish as well, and game is hunted in season.

The truffle, or 'black diamond' as it is called, occupies a special place here, for the Rhône produces more of these prized morsels than Périgord. These costly, aromatic fungi grow around *chênes truffiers*, or 'truffle oaks'. Most of these are situated in the Coteaux du Tricastin wine district in the southeastern part of the Drôme *département*, not far from Montélimar. In the first half of the 20th century, the village of Grignan alone was handling two tons of truffles a week. According to local records, even Nicolas II, last of the Russian tsars, was a customer. Truffles were the reason why, in 1937, Tricastin was not included in the Côtes du Rhône appellation: quite simply, there were more *trufficulteurs* than *viticulteurs*.

Since it can take from 15 to 20 years from planting an oak before the first truffles grow around the tree, cultivating them has become uneconomical for many farmers. Nevertheless, considerable quantities are still harvested, as can be seen in the markets at Grignan, Valréas, St-Paul-Trois-Châteaux and elsewhere. An ample supply is usually available in the season, which lasts from November to February. During this period, truffles are on the menus of most of the Rhône's restaurants, which work them into simple omelettes as well as more sophisticated dishes. St-Paul-Trois-Châteaux even has a truffle museum – the Maison de la Truffe et du Tricastin – and organises a Fête de la Truffe on the second Sunday in February.

A GREAT RANGE

Customers to Rhône restaurants are often amazed by the wide range of appetising dishes available to accompany the region's many wines. In the north, influenced by Lyon, *charcuterie* often appears on the table. Further south, the recipes take on a Provençal character, with *tapenade*, a purée of black olives, capers and olive oil, served as a starter. This 'poor man's caviar' sometimes includes anchovies or marinated tunny. Lamb is a favourite dish, often cooked with herbs; chicken comes in countless variations, including cooked with crayfish; and game appears both in classic recipes and in more subtle creations.

One Carpentras speciality is *tian*, which takes its name from an oval earthenware dish that is filled with all kinds of vegetables and some olive oil, then placed in a slow oven – a sort of variant on ratatouille. Cheeses may follow main courses; *picodon*, a goat's cheese, makes a frequent appearance. A sweet dessert rounds off the menu – nougat, perhaps, from Montélimar, or *tarte aux fruits* (fruit tart), or some other creation made with fresh fruit grown in this fertile valley.

How to use this guide

In words and pictures, this guide takes you through the entire wine region of France's Rhône Valley. The journey begins in Vienne, just below Lyon, and finishes some 200 kilometres further south in the Avignon area. Sometimes the route leaves the Rhône itself, to visit the extraordinarily beautiful Drôme Valley, for example, or to take in the wine villages at the foot of Mont Ventoux. Visits to important towns are also included: Vienne, Valence, Montélimar, Orange and Avignon are all explored. In practically every chapter a route is set out that leads through the most interesting wine villages and the most scenic areas; trunk roads are avoided as far as possible. Information on the most important sights and other items of interest has been provided for each village, including when and where local markets are held.

Where possible (and appropriate), hotels and restaurants are recommended. Some of the restaurants and cafés and many of the smaller hotels are probably not to be found in any other guide. For the most part, these are friendly, country establishments that do not cost too much, and where guests are encouraged to relax and unwind.

Of course, the best wine producers in every district and town are recommended, and represent the elite of this vast wine region. Most of them are private growers, but a number of cooperatives and wine dealers are also present in the listings sections.

HOTELS

When making a hotel reservation, always ask for a quiet room and check for any nearby church bells that are likely to ring loudly and often. When making reservations, you will usually be given a final arrival time. If you intend to arrive later, telephone the hotel; otherwise you may lose your room. It is wise to get written confirmation of any reservations. In the Rhône region, as elsewhere in France, rooms can be booked with private persons in many areas. Look for *chambres d'hôte* signs or consult the list of addresses at the town hall – known variously as the *mairie* or the *hôtel de ville* – or at the *office du tourisme* (tourist office).

RESTAURANTS

Telephone restaurants in advance to be sure of a table and to check that they are open on a particular day. Set menus generally offer the best value for money and use the freshest ingredients. In the simpler eating places it is best to choose regional dishes, as complicated recipes from elsewhere may overtax the chef. Select regional wines (local ones if possible), for they will have been more expertly and critically chosen. A carafe of tap water is always provided free.

Above *Most vineyards in the Rhône Valley tend to be small in scale – regardless of whether they belong to the most famous producers or to lesser-known growers.*

VISITING THE WINEGROWERS AND CHATEAUX

It may be difficult to see the most famous growers, particularly if they have no problems selling their wines at high prices. The less renowned, however, should welcome you with pleasure. Showing this guide may help; anyone who arrives by recommendation and appears truly interested in wine will usually be given a friendlier reception than a passing stranger.

When tasting wines – which can vary from one or two in the Côte-Rôtie to a whole range in Lirac – it is customary to spit them out, but ask first where you can do this. Ask, too, what you should do with any drops left in the glass; sometimes the producer has a special container for these. Never tip winegrowers, but do buy at least one bottle as a token of appreciation (this is unnecessary if you have paid for the visit). French is generally the only language spoken at most wineries, although nowadays many of the younger winegrowers speak English.

CHOOSING WINES TO BUY

Choosing the best wines to buy in the Rhône is not easy given the number of growers and *négociants*. Price need not reflect quality, and widely varying wines can be produced in the same village by different growers. Since winemaking methods vary, so too does wine quality. Remember: reputation counts more than price.

PLACES OF INTEREST

The Rhône is steeped in history and cultural interest. Details of the most interesting places to visit are included.

MAPS

Wine maps showing various *commune* boundaries and (where relevant) vineyard boundaries are included, complete with suggested wine routes. These routes take in the most important villages and vineyards, but if you have time, do try to explore further.

The Northern Rhône

Côte-Rôtie is the northernmost appellation in the Rhône Valley. Winegrowing on these steep, impressive slopes is nothing new: the Romans were responsible for building the terraces, or *chaillées*, which still support modern Côte-Rôtie vineyards. Yet even the Romans were not the first to plant vines here; credit for that goes almost certainly to the ancient Greeks, and either they or the Phoenicians were responsible for bringing the Syrah grape from the Middle East to this end of the valley. Syrah continues to dominate today's Côte-Rôtie vineyards, so it is not surprising that the appellation produces only red wine.

Côte-Rôtie consists of a narrow strip of winegrowing slopes situated on the west bank of the Rhône and centred around the unprepossessing town of Ampuis. The total area covered by vineyards is only 160 hectares, making the appellation's wine a fairly rare commodity. This scarcity, combined with its frequent high quality, allows Côte-Rôtie to command fairly steep prices.

Condrieu and Château Grillet, the two other wines produced in the northern Rhône, are even rarer than Côte-Rôtie. Both are exclusively white wines, and both have as their basis the exceptionally sensitive Viognier grape; in the northern Rhône's special microclimate, however, this vulnerable variety grows reasonably well. Condrieu's vineyards start immediately south of Côte-Rôtie and take in only 90 hectares, while those of tiny Château Grillet, about a kilometre further south of Condrieu, make up not quite four. Château Grillet is one of the smallest of all French appellations (although it is still larger than the 0.85 hectares of La Romanée in Burgundy).

The route through the northern Rhône Valley begins with a visit to the historic town of Vienne, before following the N86 southwards through each of the three wine

Left *Viognier vines flourish in Condrieu, one of the rarest of the Rhône appellations.*

Above *History abounds on every corner in Vienne, just a few kilometres from the Côte-Rôtie AC.*

Above *Vienne's* Jardin
Archéologique, *or archaeological
garden, contains a theatre where rites
dedicated to the goddess Cybele are
thought to have been performed.*

districts. It also points out good viewpoints from which to enjoy the scenic panorama of terraced vineyards, ancient villages and the fertile valley which surrounds the silver-blue ribbon of the River Rhône.

VIENNE

The town of Vienne makes a perfect starting point for a visit to the Rhône wine region: not only does it impart a sense of the valley's rich history, it is just a few kilometres away from the slope of the Côte-Rôtie appellation. As mentioned on page 15, the wealthy citizens of first- and second-century Vienne enjoyed the *vinum picatum* that was produced in the area, and the present 30,000 inhabitants are equally fond of their wines. The town itself stretches along the east bank of the Rhône, and since part of it is built up the slopes of Mont Pipet, many of its streets are steep.

Over 50 years before Julius Caesar conquered Gaul, the land along the Rhône which belonged to the Celtic Allobroges was subjugated by Rome, and Vienne was chosen as its capital, due to its location at the foot of the Dauphiné hills on the river's east bank. The town was thoroughly Romanised: monuments and statues were erected at the base of Mont Pipet, and its residences and shops soon extended across the Rhône to create 'suburbs' in the present-day villages of Ste-Colombe and St-Romain-en-Gal. Under the emperors Caligula and Augustus, Vienne became a prosperous centre of art and culture, and it was not long before the writers of the day were referring to the town as 'Vienne the Beautiful'.

A number of impressive monuments survive from this period. In the first century BC, a temple was built to the emperor Augustus and his wife Livia; this rectangular structure, characterised by 16 tall Corinthian columns, still stands in the centre of town on the Place du Palais. Heading southeast of the temple, a few minutes' walk leads to the *Jardin Archéologique*, (Archaeological Garden). This terraced park, situated on the Rue Victor Hugo, contains the remains of another temple as well as a theatre thought to have been dedicated to the goddess Cybele. Near the theatre stands what remains of a Roman portico, possibly the entrance to the ancient city's public baths.

East of the park (cross the Rue Victor Hugo, then follow the Montée St-Marcel to the Rue des Célestes) lies the *Théâtre Romain*. This was one of the largest amphitheatres in Roman Gaul – larger, for example, than the one at Orange. Built against the sides of Mont Pipet, its 46 rows of tiered seats could hold roughly 13,500 spectators. Today, it is used for performances in summer, including Vienne's annual jazz festival, which is held during the first fortnight in July.

On the south side of town (on the Boulevard Fernand Point) stands another Roman monument: a 23-metre-high obelisk known as *La Pyramide*. It originally marked the forecourt of the huge Vienne amphitheatre, but a medieval legend claimed that it actually stood over the tomb of Pontius Pilate, who supposedly threw himself into the Rhône in a fit of remorse. Nearby lies another 'Pyramide': the legendary restaurant made famous by Fernand Point. After a temporary decline, it is once again considered to be among the best restaurants in France.

VIENNE

HOTELS

Hôtel Central
7 Rue Archevêché
Tel: 4 74 85 18 38
An old-fashioned, reasonably comfortable hotel with 25 rooms, noisy corridors, a lift and a garage. Situated in a narrow, one-way street near the cathedral. No restaurant.

RESTAURANTS

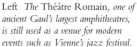

Le Bec Fin
7 Place St-Maurice
Tel: 4 74 85 76 72
This tastefully furnished restaurant is within walking distance of the Hôtel Central. It is attractively priced, with set menus that offer generous helpings and very good quality. Try the *salade Lyonnaise*. Large stock of Côte-Rôtie wines.

La Pyramide
14 Boulevard Fernand Point
Tel: 4 74 53 01 96
A top-quality restaurant that offers refined cuisine and an impressive wine list. There are also around 25 hotel rooms and suites.

Left *The* Théâtre Romain, *one of ancient Gaul's largest amphitheatres, is still used as a venue for modern events such as Vienne's jazz festival.*

More reminders of Vienne's Gallo-Roman past can be seen in the town's *Musée des Beaux-Arts et Archéologie* (Museum of Fine Arts and Archaeology), which is located on the Place de Miremont); in the public gardens which surround the *Voie Romaine*, a stretch of original Roman road complete with chariot-wheel grooves (in the Place des Allobroges), and across the Rhône in St-Romain-en-Gal, where there are extensive excavations.

Below *The Cathédrale St-Maurice, symbol of medieval Vienne's conversion to Christianity, combines both Romanesque and Gothic elements.*

Even while Rome ruled, however, a Christian community had begun to flourish in Vienne as early as the second century AD. Soon, 'Vienne the Beautiful' became known as 'Vienne the Holy', and the construction of a cathedral began in the early 12th century. This was to become the Cathédrale St-Maurice, which is set in the centre of Vienne and is surrounded by narrow streets. Despite its beginnings, however, the cathedral was not completed until the 16th century.

Above *The Temple of Augustus and Livia has played various roles over the centuries, including those of a Christian church and a law court.*

The present building is an interesting combination of Romanesque and Gothic architecture. Two towers flank the west front, whose three portals are decorated with fine carving executed in the Flamboyant Gothic style. The interior is also worth seeing, particularly for its forest of antique-style pilasters and half-fluted or twisted columns. Parts of the roof are painted, and a number of small chapels are bathed by the light filtering through the splendid stained-glass windows.

Southwest of the Cathédrale St-Maurice lies a second church that is also well worth a visit. The Ancienne Église St-Pierre is one of the oldest churches in France, and it is the burial place of the bishops of Vienne. It was constructed in the ninth century on fourth-century foundations, and the present building also incorporates sixth-century walls. Today, St-Pierre houses the *Musée Lapidaire* – the Lapidary, or Sculpture, Museum – where exhibits include an excellent collection of mosaics.

Vienne's third notable church is St-André-le-Bas, just northwest of the town centre off the Rue des Clercs. This fine Romanesque structure also has splendid cloisters, which house a collection of Christian carvings and epitaphs. The terrace by the church affords a lovely view across the river.

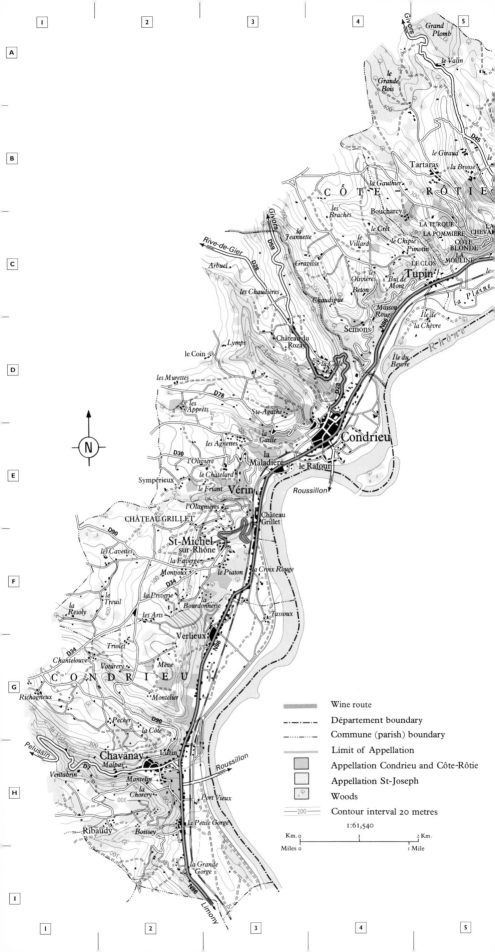

Côte-Rôtie and Condrieu

COTE-ROTIE

From Vienne, take the N7 south along the river about five kilometres, then turn right to cross the Rhône near a hydroelectric station and you enter the wine district of Côte-Rôtie. That the vines of this appellation grow on steep slopes – often on tiny terraces just a vine or two wide – is immediately apparent. This is viticulture at its most dedicated, for while the landscape provides a breathtaking experience for the tourist, its almost perpendicular, rocky face signifies sheer hard graft for the *vigneron*. While the *vignoble* is made up of three *communes* (St-Cyr-sur-le-Rhône, Ampuis and Tupin-et-Semons), it is the vineyards surrounding Ampuis, at the heart of the appellation, which are the largest and most well known. These include the renowned slopes of Côte Brune and Côte Blonde – but more of them in a moment.

The only red grape used to make Côte-Rôtie is Syrah, known locally as *Serine*, and it flourishes in the stony soil of the northern Rhône. The stones, in fact, provide a service to the vines as they soak up the sun's warmth and radiate it, even long after the sun has set for the evening. Syrah is sometimes blended with a little Viognier (up to 20 per cent is allowed), and the red wine produced by these two grape varieties is among the most celebrated in the entire Rhône Valley.

Above   *The Guigal estate in Ampuis. It was here that father and son became the first growers in the Côte-Rôtie appellation to produce single-vineyard wines – an innovation that revived what was once a sluggish wine industry.*

Above *Harvest time near Ampuis. The almost perpendicular slopes mean that picking here is still done by hand, and that the grapes must be carried down on foot.*

Far right *The sleepy little village of Ampuis is still coming to terms with the popularity its wines have achieved in the outside world.*

One sip is enough to understand why. A good Côte-Rôtie is characterised by a powerful, fruit-packed palate that shows a good deal of finesse and makes a wonderful partner for game. On the nose, it often displays a perfumed elegance, reminiscent of spring flowers, that is derived from the Viognier in the blend. It is, however, a wine that demands patience. While much of the Côte-Rôtie served in restaurants is certainly enjoyable at around just two to three years of age, usually ten to 15 years are needed in order for the wine to reveal its true greatness. Just as with any star performer, though, fame comes at a price: at its best, Côte-Rôtie can be one of most expensive Rhône wines around; to add insult to injury, many of the top *cuvées* are widely exported. Even so, you don't have to go to the most expensive producers to appreciate this wine at its best; the younger growers here have much to recommend – and they will usually be more open to visits from enthusiasts.

AMPUIS

The main village in any journey through Côte-Rôtie is Ampuis, just west of the N86. Although it is by far the appellation's most important winegrowing *commune*, Ampuis has taken its time about flirting with the outside world. Since the recent rediscovery of its wines, however, the village has begun to make an effort, smartening up its restaurants and sprouting several new shops opposite the church on the main square.

Wine, it seems, has always been a motivational factor for Ampuis. It was the wines produced here that the wealthy citizens of Vienne drank in ancient times (local artefacts include a Gallo-Roman mosaic depicting three men treading grapes), and the village remained under the archdiocese of Vienne throughout the Middle Ages. By the time of the French Revolution, Côte-Rôtie from Ampuis was exported to most of the great courts of Europe, and its fame lasted right up to the end of the 19th century.

Then, however, came the phylloxera vine louse and two world wars. The increasing industrialisation of the Rhône Valley also added to the Ampuis *vignerons*' woes by tempting the younger generations away from the village. By 1956,

RECOMMENDED PRODUCERS

Domaine Gilles Barge
Barge runs both the Côte-Rôtie growers *syndicat* as well as his own domaine. His wines are good and can be excellent, but there have been charges of inconsistency.

Domaine Bernard Burgaud
A small domaine (4ha) producing big, powerful Côte-Rôtie, using just 20% new oak without any fining or filtration.

Domaine Champet
Tiny firm (2.4ha) run by the lively and irrepressible Emile Champet and his son, Joel. Some wines are excellent, some disappointing.

Edmond Duclaux
A leading grower who began vinifying and bottling his wine in 1978.

Domaine Gentaz-Dervieux
Marius Gentaz-Dervieux produces some of the finest Côte-Rôtie from his tiny (0.42ha) Côte Brune vineyard – at much more affordable prices than the bigger names.

Etablissements Guigal
The most important Côte-Rôtie producer. Among the very top wines – top in price, too – are La Turque (Côte Brune), La Mouline (Côte Blonde) and La Landonne (Côte Brune), all single-vineyard wines which are late-harvested from tiny yields. Other Rhône wines are also of a high average quality here.

Domaine Jamet
Brothers Jean-Luc and Jean-Paul Jamet make big, exciting wines with plenty of full, fruity flavour and enough tannin to last.

Domaine Jasmin
Robert Jasmin and his son, Patrick, produce quality wines which are surprisingly elegant, if somewhat bold. Possibly too strong for delicate palates, they are nonetheless well worth seeking out.

Bernard Levet
Levet makes woody, spicy wines full of very ripe fruit.

Domaine Michel Ogier
Small, newish establishment making soft, silky wines, some from old vines. Also makes a good *vin de pays* called La Rosine.

Domaine René Rostaing
One of the larger estates, making superb smooth, spicy, consistent Côte-Rôtie with state-of-the-art equipment. Also makes fine Condrieu.

Domaine Vidal-Fleury
Since 1985, owned by E Guigal, where the wines of both firms are vinified. The domaine produces a range of Rhône wines, but the Côte-Rôtie is considered one of its best.

just over 48 hectares were in production in the entire Côte-Rôtie appellation, and 'the wine of Ampuis' had become only a distant memory.

Fortunately, it was not to stay that way for long. Cautious replanting in the 1970s gave way to a revived industry during the 1980s, led by such innovative producers as Etienne and Marcel Guigal, the father and son who struck out on their own to make some excellent single-

Below *Ampuis' position next to the Rhône meant that Côte-Rôtie was easily shipped by barge to most of the great European courts.*

vineyard wines. Due to the success of efforts such as these, around half of the appellation's maximum 500 hectares is under vine. Today's visitors to Ampuis will find signs all over the village listing directions to various producers and wine-tasting premises.

Ampuis' only real monument is Le Château, a large, Renaissance-style building situated close to the river. True to the town's unadventurous personality, though, even this is not open to the public – but its presence is significant to the wine tourist. Le Château was once home to the Maugiron family, and one of its members had two daughters – one with fair hair, the other brunette. Their father gave each of them a wine slope, and according to tradition, this is how the names *Côte Blonde* and *Côte Brune* arose. A more prosaic explanation of the names lies in the slopes' respective soils. With its greater lime content, the soil of Côte Blonde is a lighter colour than that of Côte Brune, which contains more iron. Most Côte-Rôtie wines are a blend of grapes grown on these two famous slopes, but there is a modern trend towards bottling them separately, from single vineyards. Wines from Côte Blonde tend to be finer and more elegant in structure – it is here that the more sensitive Viognier tends to be grown, after all – while those made from the grapes of Côte Brune are denser and more substantial.

TUPIN-ET-SEMONS
Guy Bernard
A Côte-Rôtie grower with a good reputation.

VERENAY
Domaine de Bonserine
This domaine belongs to the great Beaujolais firm of Georges Duboeuf.
Dervieux-Thaize
A leading Côte-Rôtie grower.
Domaine Jean-Michel Gerin
Turns out good, often excellent Côte-Rôtie, including the single-vineyard Les Grandes Places, made with 100% new wood.

RESTAURANTS

Le Côte-Rôtie
Ampuis
Tel: 4 74 56 12 05
This is an excellent establishment, offering flavourful, inventive cuisine served at astonishingly reasonable prices. The wine list includes many fine Côte-Rôtie wines.

Below *The Côte Brune vineyard. Here, the iron-rich soil yields grapes which produce substantial wines that benefit greatly from age.*

RECOMMENDED PRODUCERS

CONDRIEU

Domaine Niero-Pinchon
Young, dynamic Robert Niero makes
beautifully mature Condrieu at this
estate, as well as Côte-Rôtie and
Côtes du Rhône.

Château du Rozay
The Condrieu here is certainly in
better condition than the château
itself, which is situated on a plateau
as you head out towards Le Rozay.

Domaine Georges & Luc Vernay
Condrieu's largest estate owner,
Georges is assisted by his son, Luc.
Premises for wine tasting and sales
are located on the N86.

CHAVANAY

**Domaine de Boisseyt
(Chol et Fils)**
No Condrieu is made here,
but the domaine makes excellent
Côte-Rôtie and St-Joseph.

Yves Cuilleron
Stop here and try the superb,
vat-vinified Condrieu, Les Chaillets
Vielles Vignes. Good St-Joseph, too.

Philippe Faury
Faury produces good, complex
St-Joseph in addition to his Condrieu.

André Perret
Perret makes complex and
concentrated wines, which have
aromas of ripe apricots.

Philippe Pichon
In addition to his very agreeable
Condrieu, Pichon produces
good St-Joseph.

LIMONY

Pierre Dumazet
Dumazets have been making wine at
Limony for over 100 years, and the
estate's wines, made from low yields,
are well worth trying.

Various wine firms outside the district
also produce good Condrieu, among
them Delas Frères, E Guigal, Paul
Jaboulet Aîné and Vidal-Fleury.

WINE FAIRS AND SHOPS

● A wine shop called La Bouteillière
stands at the southern end of the
Grand Rue in Condrieu, and offers
a great range of wines, particularly
from the northern Rhône.
● End of November: *Marché aux Vins*
in Chavanay.

CONDRIEU

From Ampuis, it takes only a few minutes to drive south
along the N86 to Condrieu, the town that forms the heart
of the appellation of the same name. The white wine
produced here is one of the rarest in France – in terms of
both quality and quantity. Although Condrieu's vineyards
are spread over seven *communes* in three different
départements (Condrieu itself, in the Rhône; Limony in
the Ardèche; and Vérin, St-Michel-sur-Rhône, Chavanay,
St-Pierre de Boeuf and Malleval in the Loire), they
amounted to just 90 hectares in 1995 – a figure that is more
than ten times the area under vine in 1965.

The fortunes of Condrieu closely resemble those of
Côte-Rôtie: the appellation flourished until the end of the
19th century, then ground to a standstill during the
following two world wars. A renaissance took place during
the 1970s and 1980s, and during the early 1990s, the local
syndicat, led by producer Georges Vernay, took steps to
control yields – a shrewd and essential move, since the only

grape grown in the appellation is the temperamental Viognier. Unpredictable at the best of times, Viognier actually does fairly well here, for the windy microclimate continually ventilates the terraces, keeping the vines healthy and free from pests and mildew. Even so, most growers struggle to time their harvests correctly in order to avoid losing the perfume and *typicité* that give the resulting wine its finesse.

Just as it takes a certain degree of skill to grow Viognier, a good deal of talent is required to vinify it successfully. Years ago, it was made into both sweet and dry versions, but today's Condrieu is mainly dry. At its best, it is an agreeable, often elegant and strong white wine with a charming, rich fruitiness and an aroma that is reminiscent of ripe, juicy pears. Unlike Côte-Rôtie, however, Condrieu is designed for drinking relatively young, preferably within three years of its vintage – a testimony to the fact that most wines made from Viognier age neither well nor consistently.

Below Near the town of Condrieu, whose name means 'corner of the stream', the River Rhône takes on a decidedly more peaceful aspect.

Right Viognier grows well on the slopes of Condrieu, where winds keep pests at bay, but skill is necessary after harvest to get the best from the grapes.

HOTEL

Bellevue
Les Roches-de-Condrieu
Tel: 4 74 56 41 42
Many of the Bellevue's 20 rooms offer fine views across the river. The rooms vary in size and comfort. In the restaurant, good, fairly traditional dishes are served without too much fuss alongside good regional wines.

RESTAURANTS

Beau Rivage
Condrieu
Tel: 4 74 59 52 24
This stylish establishment by the river has antiques inside and a flower garden outside. Offers very good cuisine – rather less traditional nowadays – and an impressive wine list. Set lunch on weekdays. There are also around 25 hotel rooms and suites.
Restaurant de la Reclusière
Condrieu
Tel: 4 74 56 67 27
A small concern located on the south side of the Grand Rue, where you can eat well at reasonable prices. There is a *formule rapide* at lunchtimes which consists of the *plat du jour*, cheese or dessert and coffee. Try the *poulet fermier aux morilles* or the *filet de sandre au beurre blanc*.

The town that lends its name to this difficult character is situated on a small plateau of land which looks as if it has been wedged between the steep slopes of the west bank and the River Rhône itself. The name *Condrieu* is derived from *coin de ruisseau* – literally, 'corner of the stream' – for the town is situated on a bend in the river. Just as Condrieu itself has been compressed into its location, its centre is composed of a host of narrow, atmospheric streets, complete with a smattering of good restaurants and a few essential shops. Like its northern neighbour Ampuis, Condrieu has begun to realise the advantages of tourism: a new visitors' centre opened in 1994.

Condrieu's village atmosphere lends itself well to the pedestrian. Among its more notable sights are the remains of a feudal castle which adorn a low hill above the town. The church, in the town centre, boasts an interesting Gothic portal, but next to it stands the most beautiful building in the place: the Maison de la Gabelle. The 16th-century Maison boasts a frontage of weathered stone that is decorated with medallions and other ornate carvings – which makes it hard to believe that something as mundane as a salt tax was once collected here. The centre of Condrieu is bordered by a little stream called the Arbuel; beside it stands a former monastery.

A pleasant drive in the direction of Le Rozay leads to the local viewpoint, which offers splendid views over Condrieu, Les Roches-de-Condrieu opposite, and the river valley. This short drive could be rounded off with a visit to the pink, 17th-century Château du Rozay, where a marvellous Condrieu is made by Jean-Yves Multier.

CHATEAU GRILLET

Château Grillet is located just over a kilometre south of Condrieu, on the outskirts of St-Michel-sur-Rhône. To reach it, head south on the N86 from Condrieu, until you come to the village of Vérin. From here, turn right on the D34 in the direction of St-Michel-sur-Rhône. Immediately after a sharp bend and a small railway viaduct, you will see the terraced vineyard and the grey stone château set in what amounts to a natural amphitheatre, a beautiful site overlooking the Rhône.

Despite its close proximity to Condrieu, Château Grillet is in fact one of France's oldest and smallest appellations – even though it amounts to nothing more than a single vineyard. Much of the main château itself dates from the 17th century, but its foundations are early medieval. Whatever its origins, architecturally speaking it is frankly a somewhat less-than-beautiful mixture of styles.

The vines of the Château Grillet appellation cover just 3.8 hectares; some sprawl at the foot of the château, while others grow on surrounding terraces. Like Condrieu, the white wine made here comes solely from Viognier grapes, spends some time in wood, and then goes into slender brown bottles. Since the grapes are the same, one may well ask what makes Grillet different from Condrieu. The answer seems to lie in the soil: the vines of Château Grillet grow in a soil that contains a much higher mica content than those in other vineyards – why, no one knows for sure.

Owned by the elderly André Canet, Château Grillet has been plagued by criticism in recent years, the main charge being that the wine is not showing its full potential and that it is not equal to many less-expensive Condrieus. The better vintages, however, show subtle nuances – suggestions of flowers combined with ripe fruit. According to the owners, Château Grillet reveals its true colours with white or red meat, blue-veined cheeses and ripe peaches.

One of the oldest and smallest appellations in France, Château Grillet (above and below, left) is like a ship floating in a sea of vines. Just as in Condrieu, only Viognier is grown here, but the different soil structure produces an entirely different style of wine.

RECOMMENDED PRODUCER

Château Grillet
The only producer here. Since 1830, both château and vineyard have belonged to the Neyret-Gachet family; the current owner, André Canet, married Hélène Neyret-Gachet in 1943 and took over as manager of the château in 1961. It has been possible to trace owners of the castle back to the 17th century, but nothing is known of its earliest history. The remains of a Roman villa have been found 200 metres from the château. Besides its white wine, the estate makes a small amount of *marc* – about 100 bottles a year. Normally no wine is sold at the château, so the best way of sampling it is to order it in one of the area's top restaurants, such as Beau Rivage in Condrieu, or La Pyramide in Vienne.

The Central Rhône

Many books classify the wines of the Rhône as belonging either to the valley's northern or southern sections. While such a neat division is pleasing from a mathematician's point of view, it is in fact somewhat misleading, for it fails to take into account the unique characteristics that set the central Rhône apart from its more northerly and southerly neighbours. The wines produced here reflect the area's particular soils and microclimates, and they can vary not just from appellation to appellation, but from vineyard to vineyard – particularly in an appellation such as St-Joseph, which covers a whopping 26 different *communes*.

For the purposes of this book, then, the central Rhône wine region is best described as that part of the river valley which stretches between Chavanay (belonging to both the Condrieu and St-Joseph appellations) and the town of Valence, about 60 to 65 kilometres to the south. In contrast to the northern Rhône, some of the vineyards in this region – especially those around the town of Tain-l'Hermitage – are situated on the east as well as the west bank of the river.

To complicate matters even further, the central Rhône is home to a number of different *appellations contrôlées* and wine styles. Besides the giant Hermitage and its cousin, Crozes-Hermitage (which, for reasons of geography, will be discussed in the next chapter), these include St-Joseph – by far the most extensive of all central Rhône wine districts, and one of the most complex; Cornas, another enigmatic AC which rubs shoulders with the southern end of St-Joseph; and the tiny St-Péray, an often-overlooked AC tucked away at the central Rhône's southern limit.

Just as in the northern Rhône, Syrah is the only red grape variety grown in these appellations, but as far as white varieties are concerned, Viognier has made way

Left *The medieval château at Châteaubourg is now a splendid wine-tasting centre – which illustrates the differing fortunes of the huge St-Joseph appellation and that of tiny St-Péray (above).*

Together with his son, Pierre-Marie, Auguste Clape (right) is considered to be one of the finest producers of Cornas, the second great red wine of the central Rhône.

for two other grapes. These are Marsanne and Roussanne, which are used to enhance red wines in addition to producing whites.

In terms of quality, after Hermitage the second great red wine of the central Rhône is undoubtedly Cornas, followed by a host of wines from the districts of St-Joseph and Crozes-Hermitage. White Hermitage, too, is a giant of its kind, but there are also some engaging white wines (including some sparkling examples) to be had from Crozes-Hermitage, St-Joseph and St-Péray – although the latter is, unfortunately, a declining district.

Besides the abundant variety of wines in this part of the Rhône Valley, there is plenty to see and enjoy in the way of sights. A drive upwards through the sloping vineyards often leads to splendid panoramas, such as those from the majestic hill of Hermitage or Château de Crussol. There are ancient villages such as Malleval to be explored, and for the culturally minded, this part of the Rhône even offers a few museums, including one at Serrières devoted to inland waterways. And fortunately for the wine tourist, there is no lack of good food and drink, either.

ST-JOSEPH

The first thing one needs to realise before exploring the St-Joseph wine district is that there is no such thing as a 'typical St-Joseph' wine, either red or white. Because of its vast size – the *appellation contrôlée* stretches for about 65 kilometres – each vineyard has developed its own identity, and the wines made from the grapes growing in them have followed suit.

This was not always the case. When the St-Joseph appellation was created in 1956, it covered just six *communes* which, among them, boasted 90 hectares of vines: all were located in the Tournon area and included the town itself. In those days, the vineyards, mostly situated on sun-drenched terraces, produced wine which was considered by many to outshine Côtes du Rhône. So what happened? In 1969, the St-Joseph AC was extended to cover an area nearly four times its original length, and the number of allowable hectares ballooned to 7,000. Fortunately, only about 700 of these were actually planted before the producers realised that the new land was far better suited to growing vegetables than grapes, and the appellation was again radically restructured in 1994.

Since then, a bit more common sense has prevailed, and today's St-Joseph AC allows for a maximum of 3,004 hectares. It starts in the north in Chavanay, where it overlaps the Condrieu district, and finishes at Châteaubourg, a village that lies about halfway between the towns of Tournon and Valence. At present, only around 650 hectares are planted with vines – a reflection, perhaps, of the vignerons' more tentative approach to

Above *While not nearly so steep as the slopes of Côte-Rôtie, terraces are still the order of the day in many vineyards of the St-Joseph appellation.*

THE VILLAGES OF ST-JOSEPH

RECOMMENDED PRODUCERS

CHATEAUBOURG
Maurice & Dominique Courbis (GAEC des Ravières)
This family-run operation makes both red and white St-Joseph as well as good Cornas.

LIMONY
Louis Chèze
Produces some of the finest St-Joseph to date, both white and red. Try the Cuvée Prestige de Caroline, named for Chèze's daughter and aged in new wood.

MALLEVAL
Thierry Farjon
Farjon is known throughout the region as much for his white St-Joseph as he is for his reds.
Domaine de la Favière
Pierre Boucher's Domaine de la Favière label means a well-balanced St-Joseph with a floral nose and a velvety palate full of red-fruit flavour.

Pierre Gaillard

This talented, intensely committed grower produces splendid red and white St-Josephs, and also makes a fine Viognier and Côte Rôtie.

MAUVES

Domaine Pierre Coursodon

Coursodon is considered by many to be a master of both red and white St-Joseph. His 'Paradis' label is certainly well worth trying.

Pierre Gonon

Gonon produces well-structured red and white St-Joseph.

Domaine Bernard Gripa

Bernard Gripa is a conscientious producer of distinguished wines, both red and white. Mostly St-Joseph, but Gripa also makes a fine St-Péray.

ST-DESIRAT

Cave Coopérative de St-Désirat

The local co-op produces balanced, well-made red and white St-Josephs.

ST-JEAN-DE-MUZOLS

Delas Frères

Wholesale firm that also has its own vineyards in various Rhône districts. The red François de Tournon is a successful St-Joseph.

Raymond Trollat

Trollat's 2ha of wines yield what many consider to be some of the best examples of consistently good red and white St-Joseph.

ST-PIERRE-DE-BOEUF

Alain Paret

Paret's fortunes took a turn for the better when actor Gérard Depardieu tasted his wine and liked it enough to become a partner in the business. Noteworthy wines include the red cuvée Les Larmes du Père, but try his Côtes du Rhône and the fine Condrieu Les Ceps du Nébadon.

ST-VALLIER

L de Vallouit

This energetic producer operates a tasting centre situated in the castle at Châteaubourg. He also has an estate and makes red St-Joseph Les Anges and other wines.

winemaking that has been learned from bitter experience. The heart of the appellation still revolves around these original six *communes*.

More than 90 per cent of the present production of St-Joseph consists of red wine, usually made exclusively from Syrah; however, the addition of some white grapes is allowed. Styles – and quality – vary considerably from young, easy-drinking wines to skilfully treated reds which show a depth and complexity similar to that of red Hermitage. At its best, red St-Joseph is supple and firm, with a meaty taste and plenty of fruit. It can be drunk young, but when well made, has enough backbone to last a decade or longer. However, some uninteresting St-Josephs are also marketed; these lack personality and are sometimes dour and rustic.

In the white category, the best examples (made chiefly from Marsanne) tend to be the youngest and freshest; too many white St-Josephs are old, flacid, and dull. Even so, good wines are waiting to be discovered. Choose reputable producers and you will not be disappointed.

The name 'St-Joseph' was taken from a vineyard situated between Tournon and the town of Mauves, not far to the south. The vineyard, which was first mentioned

Right *The once-fortified village of Malleval has changed very little since its construction. Most of the houses date from the 16th century.*

in the 17th century, still exists (beside the N86); most of it belongs to the firm of Chapoutier, which stakes its claim with a large signboard.

Winemaking in this area has had a much longer history than this vineyard, however, and wine from the St-Joseph appellation used to be known as *vin de Mauves* – 'the wine of Mauves'. It is referred to as such in *Les Misérables*, by Victor Hugo (1802-1885): 'My brother had him drink the good wine of Mauves, which he does not drink himself, for he says that it is too expensive.' Fortunately for today's consumer, the expense has gone down, and the roughly 50 growers are striving to bring the 'good' back into all the 'wines of Mauve'.

THE VILLAGES OF ST-JOSEPH

Follow the N86 south past Chavanay to the village of St-Pierre-de-Boeuf; the *Boeuf*, which means 'ox or bullock', was originally *Bois* ('wood'), but no one seems to know just why or how the name was changed. Viticulture has been practised here since at least the 11th century, and the village served as a port from which wine used to be shipped down the Rhône to the papal cellars at Avignon.

SARRAS
Cave Coopérative de Sarras
The Cuvée Champtenaud made by this co-op is among the best red St-Josephs around.

TOURNON
Bernard Faurie
Known more for his Hermitage, Faurie also makes both red and white St-Joseph.
Jean-Louis Grippat
Although he also makes Hermitage, Grippat is best known for his stylish, delicious St-Joseph wines, both red and white.

WINE FESTIVALS AND TASTINGS
● Last weekend before May 1: wine fair in Malleval. There is also a shop in the village that sells locally distilled drinks as well as wines.

HOTELS
Le Château Hôtel de Paris
Tournon
Tel: 4 75 08 60 22
The rooms may look old-fashioned, but all 14 are provided with modern comforts, and there is also a restaurant. The hotel is situated on the quay beside the Rhône, and offers a small garage.
Interhôtel Les Amandiers
Tournon
Tel: 4 75 07 24 10
This modern, functional hotel is located on the main road to Mauves. It offers 25 rooms, but no restaurant.
Le Mallaviot
Malleval
Tel: 4 74 87 10 51
An unpretentious establishment with 5 comfortable rooms.
Schaeffer
Serrières
Tel: 4 75 34 00 07
The owners have carried out many improvements here in recent years. All 15 rooms have been wholly renovated, and also fitted with double glazing – not a luxury, given the traffic on the quay outside. A good place to stay for stylish ambience and cheerful colours. You can also eat extremely well in the restaurant, where ingredients fresh from the market are prepared with care and talent. There is also a good list with regional wines.

RESTAURANTS

Hostellerie La Diligence
St-Pierre-de-Boeuf
Tel: 4 74 87 12 19
Located beside the busy N86, behind a shady tree, the Diligence offers fairly traditional, quality cooking based on fresh produce.

Hôtel Azalées
Tournon
Tel: 4 75 08 05 23
You can eat local dishes full of flavour at reasonable prices in this simple hotel, which is located in the Avenue de la Gare. Choose from over 30 comfortable rooms.

LOCAL ATTRACTIONS

● A small Wednesday market is held in St-Pierre-de-Boeuf.
● During the holiday season, take a ride on the tiny steam train which leaves Tournon every morning for Lamastre. The return trip lasts four hours, and runs through the romantic Doux Valley.

Below The village of Tournon-sur-Rhône. Just as in Mauves to the south, the wines of Tournon were once praised in royal circles.

Visually, St-Pierre-de-Boeuf does not have a great deal to offer; nearby Malleval has considerably more, so head for it by turning right onto the D503 at the restaurant known as La Diligence. The road leads through the deep and sinister-sounding Malleval gorge; the name literally means 'valley of evil', but these days there is nothing remotely evil about the place. After passing by the scenic Saut de Laurette waterfall on the right, turn right onto a narrow lane (it will eventually become the D79) that leads up into the village itself.

Malleval is situated on a rocky spur near the confluence of two streams, in a valley that links the River Rhône with the Vivarais. It is a village that is best seen on foot, so park on the square and walk through its quiet streets. In the early days, because of its strategic location, a castle was built in Malleval, and its presence attracted conflict. Thus, in 1574, it was set ablaze by Protestants during one of the French religious wars. Although the Catholics managed to retake the castle, they subsequently neglected it. In a direct line with the castle ruins (the medieval keep remains) stands a Romanesque church.

On the east side of the village stands a building known as *le petit château*, a beautiful little structure that was spared destruction in the wars of the 16th century. The same is true of the medieval salt market, which is situated near the castle keep. Wine can be tasted and bought in Malleval, and a workshop for drying flowers has also been established here.

For a wonderful view over Malleval and the gorge, you can either drive out in the direction of Pélussin, parking just after going round a sharp, left-hand bend, or you can drive back through the village, turning right on the D503 and

Above *Most of the grapes grown in the St-Joseph appellation are Syrah, which is the main variety used in the majority of red wines.*

head up to the 'official' viewpoint. Bear in mind that coming back from the village takes longer than driving there, since traffic has been diverted.

Once back on the N86, head south to Limony, a good example of how even the most unpretentious village in the Rhône has an historic story to tell. In the centre, near the village church, stands a Roman column about two metres high. Tradition states that it was erected in memory of a slave girl who had been raised as a daughter by a Roman couple, but, tragically, died young.

Back on the N86, drive on southwards for about four kilometres until you reach the larger village of Serrières, where a suspension bridge spans the River Rhône. This is an old bargemen's town, so it is fitting that it is home to the *Musée des Mariniers du Rhône* (the Rhône Bargemen's Museum). The museum resides in the former St Sornin's chapel at the southern end of town, where it was established in 1938. The bargemen were known as *culs-de-piau*, or 'leather-bottoms', due to their leather-lined trousers, and besides displaying some of their humble mementos – including hammers, pincers, jugs and lanterns – the museum also features a number of boatmen's crosses. These figures, naively decorated with emblems of the Passion, adorned the prows of each barge and were thought to protect the crews from the hazards of the wild Rhône. The museum also contains a reconstructed 19th-century grocer's shop, an old kitchen and a charnel house.

Above *At their best, vineyards such as this one, owned by Maurice Courbis, should produce red St-Josephs which are supple and firm, and whites which are lively and fresh.*

Further south along the N86, about six kilometres, the next town of any significance is Champagne, which has nothing to do with northern France's famous fizzy region. It can be recognised from afar by its impressive church, a 12th-century structure dedicated to St Peter. The interior in particular is very beautiful and harmonious – worth a stop, if you're in the mood – and the church is the only one in the Rhône to have a nave vaulted with a series of domes on squinches. If viewing architecture has worked up a thirst, the nearby town of St-Désirat, reached by turning right on the D291 just outside Champagne, has a dynamic wine cooperative (located right next to the N86), a fruit growers' cooperative, and a distillery which produces fruit brandies.

Andance, the next village along the N86, lies at the foot of some granite 'needles', or rock formations, and boasts the oldest existing suspension bridge in France. The bridge dates from 1827 and links Andance with the village of Andancette on the opposite bank of the Rhône. One of the region's rare Gothic churches is located in Andance; in its right chapel is a remarkable crew's cross, another legacy of life on the river.

Continue heading south along the N86 towards Sarras, the next village. Along the way, the road leads past a ruined Roman sarcophagus known as *La Sarrasinière d'Andance*. It is about ten metres long and built of dark-coloured stone.

When in Sarras, which is roughly six kilometres from Andance, it is worth crossing the Rhône on the D86 over to St-Vallier, where the château of the counts of Poitiers still stands. While the château itself is not open to the public, various spots around St-Vallier offer good views.

Cross back over the Rhône to Sarras, and continue your southerly progression along the N86. This is the Rhône Valley at its most medieval: remains of fortresses and defence towers line both banks – legacies of more violent times – and when you come to Arras-sur-Rhône, you'll find that its tower is matched by a rival one across the river at Serves-sur-Rhône.

Some seven kilometres further along lies St-Jean-de-Muzols, where the wine firm of Delas Frères is established. The winegrowing theme continues in the local church, located in the old part of the village, where the head of a man with grapes hanging from his moustache can be seen on the apsidal arch.

From St-Jean-de-Muzols, it is only a short drive south to Tournon-sur-Rhône, a busy town with a population of about 9,000. The most notable thing to see is the 15th- to 16th-century château close to the riverside. For a long time, the building served as a prison; today it houses a small museum of working life on the Rhône. Even if the museum doesn't appeal, visit the château terraces: there is a marvellous view across the river of the hill of Hermitage and the town of Tain-l'Hermitage.

Nearby, but situated on a lower level than the castle, stands the St-Julien collegiate church, which is worth visiting for its collection of murals and paintings. Its interior contains various examples of the Flamboyant Gothic style, such as in the choir and the Pénitents' chapel, and the coffered ceiling is especially appealing.

The centre of Tournon consists of steep streets, some of which are now pedestrianised. It is home to France's oldest *lycée*, or secondary school: the Lycée Gabriel-Faure, which was founded in 1536 and rebuilt in the 18th century. Its attractive Renaissance doorway leads to a collection of tapestries and busts.

The next-to-last village on our tour of the St-Joseph wine district is Mauves, around three kilometres south of Tournon, just off the N86. Contrary to the sound of its name, Mauves is a rather colourless village. By far the most notable building is the church, on the roof of which once stood a huge figure of Christ; this was struck by lightning, however, and now only the head remains, positioned in front of the door. A good time to visit Mauves is when the fruit market is held – early on Wednesday mornings during the season.

Back on the N86, head south for around five kilometres to the village of Châteaubourg, where our journey ends. Châteaubourg is dominated by a medieval château, perched high on a hill above the town. Although it has played various roles over the years – including that of a restaurant – nowadays the castle is a wine-tasting and sales centre for the firm of L de Vallouit.

Below *The bustling little town of Tournon-sur-Rhône is ideal for sightseeing on foot, as many of its steep streets are pedestrianised. Across the River Rhône, Tain-l'Hermitage (bottom) is home to some of the region's most famous* négociant *firms.*

Right The town of Cornas is easily recognisable by its uncharacteristically high church tower. Otherwise, it remains a quiet, rather unremarkable village – despite the fact that it produces some of the best red wine of the Rhône. Most of the vineyards, such as this one belonging to Jean-Luc Colombo (below right), climb up hillsides which overlook the town itself.

RECOMMENDED PRODUCERS

Domaine Thierry Allemand
One of Cornas' younger winemakers, Allemand makes wines from low yields; as a result, they are softer than many, but show a great depth of fruit. He also makes some St-Joseph, which he sells to the local co-op.

Domaine Guy de Barjac
One of the most renowned winegrowers in Cornas, de Barjac uses no new wood to make his wines – the tannins prove too much for the style – some of which age well for up to 10 years or more.

**Domaine Auguste &
Pierre-Marie Clape**
Auguste is the father, Pierre-Marie the son. Together, these Clapes make exemplary wines year in, year out, which benefit from age. Even the ordinary table wine, Le Vin des Amis, is a treat. The Clape cellar is situated in Cornas beside the N86, opposite the Ollier restaurant.

Jean-Luc Colombo
The outspoken Colombo caused consternation among older growers when he first arrived here in the early '80s, but his deeply fruity wines put paid to the local critics – even if they still don't suffer him gladly. Try the Les Terres Brulées, made from 30- to 50-year-old vines.

Dumien-Serrette
This estate produces a ruby-coloured wine with an aroma of violets and cassis, and a balanced palate that is built to last.

Domaine Marcel Juge
A talented, committed producer, who still chooses foot-treading over machine-pressing. His best wines are the cuvées 'C' and 'SC': lighter than many, more elegant than most.

Domaine Jean Lionnet
One of the largest producers in Cornas (Lionnet has 10ha), who also makes a fine St-Péray. His Cornas is perhaps more oaky than most, but no less impressive for that.

CORNAS

About four kilometres on the N86 are all that separate the town of Châteaubourg in the St-Joseph appellation from the village and wine district of Cornas to the south, but the two ACs could hardly be more different. For a start, Cornas is much smaller: while the delimited *vignoble* allows for 550 hectares, only about 90 are currently under vine. The vineyards form a steep, often terraced amphitheatre to the west of the village itself, and the soils range from a mixture of limestone, clay and granite in the south to mainly granite soils in the lower, western sites, a *terroir* that gives the AC its individual style. This sheltered position means that a drier and warmer microclimate prevails in Cornas than in the surrounding area, and the cold *mistral* has less effect on its vineyards – all of which, of course, benefits the development of the Syrah grapes (the only grape allowed for Cornas), and gives the resulting wine a meaty, earthy flavour.

Wine from *Cornatis* or *Cornatico* was mentioned from the ninth century onwards; Charlemagne is said to have drunk it in 840, and references occur in texts from the 14th, 18th and 19th centuries. At first, there was mention of white as well as red wine, but today, of course, only the latter is made. Qualitatively, Cornas is among the best of the Rhône

Valley wines, a factor which is sometimes reflected in its price – though, happily, not to the same extent as in Côte-Rôtie. In their youth, the best examples possess a hearty, robust flavour, with plenty of fruit as well as darker elements such as chocolate and tar. Give the same wines ten years or so, however, and they take on an air of elegance and complexity (not to mention more refined raspberry and brambly fruit) that makes them well worth the effort of finding space in the cellar.

The village that lends its name to this appellation lies on the N86, an unremarkable community dominated by an unusually high church tower which rises some 52 metres. The remains of a Roman villa have been found in Cornas, and it is probable that winegrowing here dates from the same period. While new housing for Valence commuters has gone up, particularly in the north of the village, Cornas' old centre still consists of narrow streets, rather colourless houses and a couple of squares which boast the usual essential shops. The only real feature of interest – apart from the wine, of course – is the 12th-century chapel of Notre-Dame de la Mure de la Vierge Noire, where a figure of the Virgin Mary is worth seeing. A short drive along the small, winding road that leads westward to St-Romain-de-Lerps offers a fine view over the whole of Cornas, with Valence in the distance.

Returning to the N86, a short drive south of about two kilometres takes you to St-Péray, the last village and AC in our tour of the central Rhône.

Domaine Robert Michel
Makes a definitely masculine, rugged Cornas with a good concentration of fruit.

Domaine Noël Verset
An octogenarian winemaker who still works 1.94ha of vines – some of which are as old as he is. The result of the wisdom of age is a generous, round, traditional style of Cornas which benefits from keeping.

Domaine Alain Voge
Another of Cornas' larger wine-growers, with 7ha of vines in Cornas, and 4ha in St-Péray. The latter is fine, and the Cornas can be excellent. Try the Vieille Fontaine – *if* you can find it.

WINE FAIRS AND FESTIVALS

● First Sunday in December: a wine market is held in Cornas.

RESTAURANT

Ollier
Tel: 4 75 40 32 17
Country restaurant situated on the N86 and furnished in rustic style. Serves appetising dishes at very reasonable prices. Specialities include *chèvreau au vin blanc* (young goat in white wine); another is leg of hare in mature Cornas.

Above *St-Péray once basked in the glory earned by its sparkling wines, but today its reputation – such as it is – is based on the still wines produced by local growers, many of whom have to make Cornas to earn a living. Even so, most of the vineyards (right) that remain are planted with Marsanne.*

RECOMMENDED PRODUCERS

ST-PERAY

Jean-François Chaboud
One of the most famous and biggest producers of sparkling and still St-Péray. It was an ancestor of Chaboud, the wine merchant Louis-Alexandre Faure, who made the first sparkling St-Péray by the *méthode champenoise* in 1829. Today, Chaboud's wines are excellent and complex – a real memorial to Faure.

Pierre Darona & Fils
Darona is one of the more important sparkling-wine producers, situated on the road to Toulaud.

Domaine de Fauterie
Sylvain Bernard produces delicious Cornas in addition to his St-Péray.

Maison Cotte Vergne
This estate produces a generous, aromatic still wine with a perfect relationship between price and quality.

Jean Teysseire & Fils
Try the still and sparkling St-Péray.

TOULAUD

Jean-Louis Thiers
The hamlet of Toulaud comes within the St-Péray appellation, even though it lies 6km further south on the D279. Here, Jean-Louis Thiers makes a delightful sparkling St-Péray, as well as a honeyed *tranquille*. There is a reasonable Cornas, too.

ST-PERAY

In 1877, Richard Wagner (1813-1883) wrote a letter to Maison Chapoutier in which he asked for 100 bottles of dry, sparkling St-Péray to be sent to him at Bayreuth, where he was composing the opera *Parsifal*. At the time, the wine was famed far beyond France, and was considered to be the country's best sparkling wine after Champagne. Half a century later, a dozen wine firms were still active in St-Péray, together producing a million bottles of sparkling wine a year. (*Tranquille*, or still, St-Péray was famous much earlier, as is clear from 16th-century references.)

Sadly, little is left of that former glory today. Total vineyard area in St-Péray has shrunk to a minuscule 65 hectares (1,900 are allowed); most of the wine firms have gone, and the reputation of the wines themselves has been almost forgotten. Only a few producers make really good St-Péray (sparkling or *tranquille*), and many of these produce Cornas for a living. Marsanne is the chief grape, although some producers are now experimenting increasingly with Roussanne. The demise of this little region is a real shame, particularly as many of the still wines are worth drinking and good value – and they are better than most white

Pôle 2000
Tel: 4 75 40 55 56
A modern, functional and (frankly) slightly dull hotel, but with adequate comfort. It is situated on the road to Valence, and offers a choice of 25 rooms. The restaurant features very affordable set menus.

RESTAURANTS

Badet
Tel: 4 75 81 04 87
This brasserie, situated by a road junction, is easily recognisable by the two giant bottles which loom at the entrance. It's suitable for a simple lunch or a drink, and it also offers simple – and noisy – hotel rooms.
Hôtel de la Gare
Tel: 4 75 40 30 06
You can eat well in the hotel's restaurant – and, of course, it also has 15 unpretentious hotel rooms.

St-Josephs. Wines made from old vines are generally best, and some producers have created oaked versions which are always the first to sell out on the local market.

The town of St-Péray itself consists of an oval-shaped nucleus to which new districts have been added in all directions – a typical victim of urban sprawl. Still, the old part of town boasts a pleasant, tree-lined square by the town hall, made more picturesque by the bells on its roof.

Park in the square and head for the nearby summit of the Crussol mountain range for the literal 'high point' of any visit to St-Péray. Here you will find a splendid viewpoint at the remains of the early medieval Château de Crussol, a once-mighty fortress; even as a ruin, it is still imposing. On the way, you will pass the 17th-century Château de Beauregard (not open to the public), and halfway up the slope you can rest by an enormous white statue of the Virgin Mary. As you reach the summit with its magnificent view, be aware that you are following in the footsteps of greatness: Napoleon made this same walk on various occasions when he was encamped in Valence, and he was often accompanied by his brother Joseph, who would later become the king of Spain.

Hermitage and the
Die Country

Given the astonishing array of wine appellations and *communes* found along the west bank of the central Rhône Valley, at first glance the east bank seems almost bland by comparison. Look closely, however, and you will find that nothing could be further from the truth: the east bank is the home of Hermitage, a name that causes many a modern wine-lover to adopt a reverential air. Red Hermitage is considered the most powerful Syrah-based wine in the Rhône; white Hermitage, too, has its admirers, many of whom contend that – in the right hands – it is even better than the red. Add to these two giants the 'junior' appellation of Crozes-Hermitage, whose red and white wines vary from easy-drinkers to powerful Hermitage contenders, and you have an area which more than makes up in quality what it lacks in quantity. As such, it is a natural stop for any wine tourist.

Or indeed for tourists of any type, for the landscape in this part of the Rhône is as powerful and breathtaking as its wines. The two appellations stretch from Serves-sur-Rhône in the north to Pont-de-l'Isère in the south, a section of the valley filled with ruins of castles and defensive towers which provide a glimpse into the turbulent Rhône Valley of the Middle Ages. The most striking sight in the whole area, however, is undoubtedly the astonishing hill of Hermitage: a huge, grey, largely granite rock which thrusts upwards from the surrounding countryside, forcing even the mighty Rhône itself to change its course eastwards in a dramatic curve just above the town of Tournon on the opposite bank.

It is here, at the hill of Hermitage, that the tour of one of the finest wine regions in France begins. Following that is an excursion into the scenic Die Country east of the Rhône, a region which has plenty of wines of its own to discover.

Left and above It began with a hermit – at least according to legend. In any case, a chapel has stood on the hill of Hermitage for centuries, keeping watch over the vineyards which produce some of the finest wine in France.

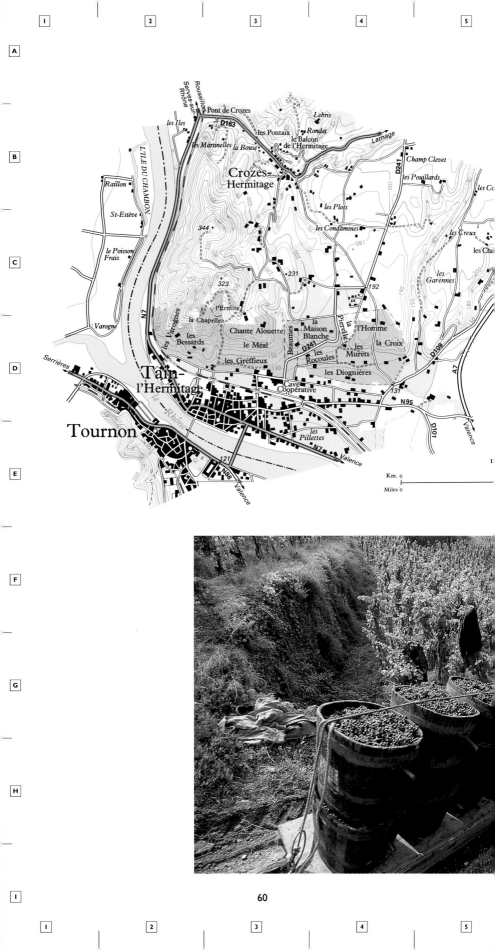

Roussillon
Serves-sur-Rhône
Pont de Crozes
les Iles
D163
les Pontaix
Lebris
Rondet
le Balcon
de l'Hermitage
Larnage
les Martinelles
la Bouse
Crozès-Hermitage
D241
Champ Clevet
les Pouillards
Raillon
L'ÎLE DU CHAMBON
les Plois
les Condamines
les Creux
les Ch
St-Estève
344
081
les Garennes
le Poisson Frais
250
231
192
190
323
l'Ermite
la Chapelle
Chante Alouette
la Maison Blanche
la Pierelle
l'Homme
la Croix
Varogne
N7
les Varognes
les Bessards
le Méal
Beaumes
D241
les Rocoules
les Murets
A7
les Gréffieux
les Diognières
D109
Serrières
Tain-l'Hermitage
Cave Coopérative
131
N95
le Rhône
D101
Valence
Tournon
les Pillettes
N7
Valence
121
N86
Valence

Km. 0
Miles 0

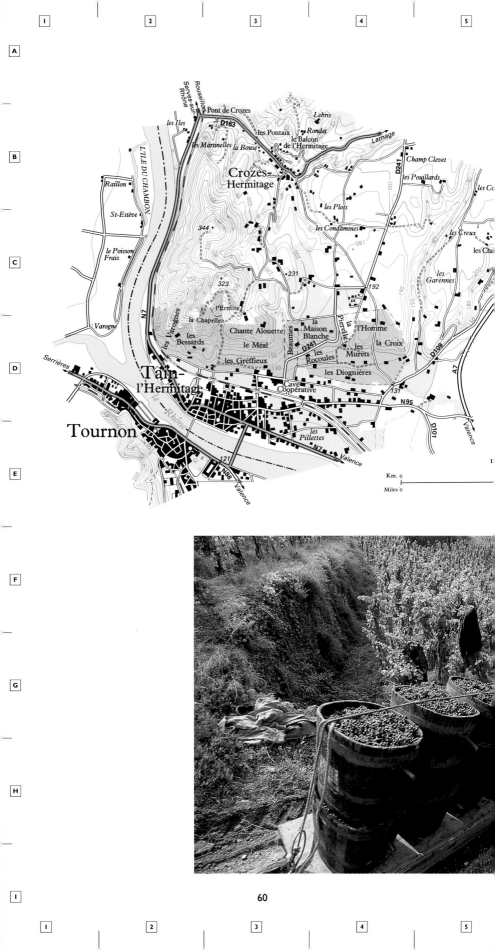

Hermitage and Crozes-Hermitage

—·—·—·— Département boundary

Appellation Contrôlée Hermitage

Appellation Contrôlée Crozes-Hermitage

Woods

——200—— Contour interval 10 metres

Wine route

2 Km.

1 Mile

THE HILL OF HERMITAGE

The first vines on the southern flanks of the 273-metre-high hill were probably planted in the fourth century BC. At any rate, archaeologists know from excavations that vines were certainly being grown in Hermitage during Roman times – as well they might, for the conditions here are perfect for them. The steep, southern slope of the hill provides some 150 hectares of terraced granite which retains the warmth of the sun and allows rainwater to drain away quickly. It is an ideal combination that has allowed the vines in this area, and the grapes that grow from them, to remain healthy throughout the centuries.

Little wonder, then, that the wines of *Tegna* (as Tain-l'Hermitage was originally known) were praised by the ancient Romans during the first century AD, but it was not until the 16th century that 'Hermitage' as a name came into common use. Legend has it that Henri Gaspard de Sterimberg, a 13th-century crusader, came to the hill after the wars ended to live the rest of his life as a hermit – hence the name. Whether or not the legend is strictly true, a small, early medieval chapel still stands on the summit of the Hermitage hill; today, it belongs to the firm of Paul Jaboulet Aîné, which illuminates it at night and uses it on its 'Hermitage La Chapelle' wine label.

Left *Harvest on the hill.*
Vineyards have grown on the
southern side of the hill of
Hermitage since pre-Christian times.

TAIN-L'HERMITAGE

RECOMMENDED PRODUCERS

Paul Jaboulet Aîné
The family-run firm of Jaboulet makes a red Hermitage, La Chapelle, that is considered one of the world's greatest wines; it will often mature for decades. Other wines (including St-Joseph, Cornas and Condrieu) are of a brilliantly high quality.

Cave Coopérative de Tain-l'Hermitage
More than 600 members of the co-op bring in over 25% of the grapes used for Hermitage wines to this reliable, quality-minded establishment. In addition, 65% of all Crozes-Hermitage is vinified here, plus 35% of St-Péray, 15% of Cornas, and 10% of St-Joseph.

Chapoutier
This large concern is the biggest owner of the Hermitage vineyards; the 31ha it works also include rented land. The firm is a family affair, run by brothers Marc and Michel, who also own vineyards in other Rhône wine districts, including Crozes-Hermitage, St-Joseph and Côte-Rôtie. The quality of all the wines offered by the Chapoutiers is exceptionally reliable – a result, perhaps, of the fact that all their vineyards are run on a biodynamic basis. Try the *têtes de cuvées*: Ermitage Le Pavillon for red, Cuvée l'Orée for white.

Gérard et Jean-Louis Chave
Another family operation, this time consisting of father (Gérard) and son. Renowned in particular for red and white Hermitage. The white is made up of roughly 85% Marsanne, 15% Roussanne, harvested from 60-year-old vines. The smallest detail receives attention here – and it shows.

Michel Ferraton
Ferraton's style is not to everyone's taste – some call his wines coarse, others won't buy anything else.

Domaine Jean-Michel Sorrel
Run by one of a pair of brothers not always on the best of terms, this estate nonetheless produces some wonderful wine, particularly the red Hermitage.

Domaine Marc Sorrel
Brother to the above, making fine Hermitage and white Crozes-Hermitage. Try Le Gréal, made from a blend of older vines.

WINE FAIRS AND FESTIVALS

● Third Sunday in September: annual wine festival in Tain-l'Hermitage. A wine competition is also held at the same time.

Whatever its exact origins, by the 17th century Hermitage was known and enjoyed throughout the courts of Europe. During the decades that followed, it went from strength to strength, as well as from country to country. In the 18th century, English writer Henry Fielding (1707-1754) mentioned Hermitage in his novel *Tom Jones*; the wine was also served to Cardinal Richelieu, and it was well known at both the French and the Russian courts. In addition, Hermitage was used in the 18th and 19th centuries to add structure to many famous Bordeaux wines.

Modern red Hermitage remains a remarkable, chiefly pure-Syrah wine that combines colour, strength and tannin in a formidable combination, and has an almost legendary lifespan. Fruit is present as a rule – blackberries, currants, cherries – and there can be a slight smokiness on the palate, as well as hints of wood. Like a good vintage port, red Hermitage needs to be decanted, since it throws a heavy sediment in the bottle. When young, it is quite closed and tannic, but with age, its perfume and full, fruity flavour become almost overwhelming.

White Hermitage, too, is impressive and represents roughly a quarter of total production. It comes in various styles, but at its best, it is a rich, generous wine with a floral perfume and an almost exotic aroma of spices and flint. The grapes used are Marsanne (sometimes 100 per cent) and Roussanne.

With two wines such as these being made in the neighbourhood, it is no wonder that the tiny town of Tain-l'Hermitage has become a place of pilgrimage for wine-lovers.

Left Tain-l'Hermitage, as seen from the River Rhône. Wine has been produced in and around this bustling village since Roman times – as witnessed by written accounts left by the ancient Romans themselves. Far left Red Hermitage is made primarily from Syrah grapes such as these, but some producers add a low percentage of white grapes to produce a wine of greater finesse.

HOTELS

Hôtel Les 2 Coteaux
Tel: 4 75 08 33 01
Situated in a quiet location on the quay near the suspension bridge, the hotel offers 20 comfortable rooms, but no restaurant.

Mercure
Tel: 4 75 08 65 00
The Mercure provides four-star comfort in the main street, with around 50 rooms kitted out with modern furnishings. You can also sample some good, fairly traditional cooking here, and there is a swimming pool, a terrace and a wine-tasting room.

RESTAURANTS

La Grappe d'Or
Tel: 4 75 08 28 52
A genial, straightforward little place on the corner of the north side of the main street. Try the three-course set menu.

Reynaud
Tel: 4 75 07 22 10
Situated on the south side of Tain on the N7 and named after its owner and chef, Jean-Marc Reynaud. In the stylish, classically furnished dining room you can try excellent dishes, often based on ingredients from the region. There is a four-course set menu, *La Cuisine du Marché*. The Reynaud is also a hotel with around 10 pleasant rooms (some with a view of the river) and a swimming pool.

Rive Gauche
Tel: 4 75 07 05 90
Ideal for guests at Les 2 Coteaux (see hotels) for it is situated opposite, in a new building. Fine dishes are prepared by a talented chef, and served in a dining room that commands a view of the Rhône.

LOCAL ATTRACTIONS

● A narrow, winding road leads to the Hermitage chapel up the hill's northern slope, where the panoramic view is magnificent.

TAIN-L'HERMITAGE

Tain-l'Hermitage is situated between the hill of Hermitage itself and the River Rhône, on either side of the N7. It is a bustling little town with a population of around 5,000, and it boasts a long history dating back to before Roman times.

In the main street stands a low granite block known as the *taurobole,* which, in the second century Roman settlement of *Tegna,* served as an altar for sacrificing bulls. The *taurobole* is situated in front of a small tasting stall shaped like a wine press – a testament to the fact that Tain serves as the general centre of trade for much of the east bank's wines. Several *négociants* and producers have their offices here, including the famous firms of Chapoutier and Paul Jaboulet Aîné (signs in the main street point the way), as well as an excellent wine cooperative, located towards the hill across the railway lines. These producers carry a large selection of wines, but Hermitage is the undisputed star of their ranges.

Among the other charms of Tain are its charming riverside quays, partly tree-lined, which make a very pleasant spot for a relaxing walk and offer a fine view of Tournon across the river (*see* page 52). For the more energetic, it is possible to walk from here to Tournon by means of a rather rickety old suspension bridge which has been barred to motor traffic.

RECOMMENDED PRODUCERS

CROZES-HERMITAGE

Michel Martin
One of the leading growers of Crozes-Hermitage – and one of the few who is actually based there.

BEAUMONT-MONTEUX

Cave des Clairmonts
This co-op has the reputation of turning out good wines even in the most difficult vintages. The 1992 is beautifully soft.

CHANOS-CURSON

Château de Curson/ Domaine Pochon
Young Etienne Pochon makes some full-bodied, flavourful Crozes at this estate, as well as releasing wine under his own Domaine Pochon label.

Domaine des Entrefaux
The Crozes here has a spicier tang than many. Good, exciting wines.

Domaine Pradelle
Brothers Jacques and Jean-Louis Pradelle make reliable red Crozes which displays an aroma of exotic fruits and a well-balanced palate.

EROME

Robert Rousset
Rousset produces both red and white Crozes, as well as a sparkling wine.

GERVANS

Domaine Fayolle
The estate produces beautifully harmonious red Crozes.

Raymond Roure
Once this estate made some of the best Crozes around, but the wines have been going through a recent patchy phase. Still, the elderly Roure is capable of producing some superb wine, especially red.

LARNAGE

Albert Belle
Besides his full, rich Crozes, Albert Belle also makes a good, gutsy Hermitage.

CROZES-HERMITAGE

Look northwards from the hill of Hermitage, in the opposite direction of Tain-l'Hermitage and Tournon, and you will see a green, rolling landscape with white farmsteads and a few small villages. This is part of the Crozes-Hermitage appellation, which began in 1937 with just one *commune*.

Since then, it has grown somewhat. New legislation in the 1950s upgraded vineyards previously classified as Côtes du Rhône, and today's Crozes-Hermitage AC boasts an official 4,200 hectares, with around 1,200 of those currently under vine – an area almost eight times the size of Hermitage. The appellation forms a sort of rough triangle around the town of Tain-l'Hermitage (which is included in it). Serves-sur-Rhône is the most northerly of its 11 *communes*, Pont-de-l'Isère the southernmost, with the distance in between around 25 kilometres. Approximately 90 per cent of Crozes-Hermitages is red, made exclusively from Syrah grapes, although rules allow up to 15 per cent of white grapes to be used at the fermentation stage.

Right *Château de Curson.*
This and other estates have been responsible for raising the standards of Crozes-Hermitage in recent years.

Prior to the early 1980s, Crozes-Hermitage was – well, frankly, not much to write home about. Most of the wine (red or white) was flabby and thin, having nothing more than part of its name in common with its superior cousin on the other side of the hill. Fortunately, a number of the winegrowers and domaines in the region began to improve the quality of Crozes, and their efforts have, on the whole, been wonderfully successful. Modern Crozes often boasts a robust taste with delightful, berry-like fruit and (often) a touch of oak. While many of the reds can mature into complex, even gamey wines, their fruit-packed palates make them hard to resist when young. In line with red Crozes, the standard of white Crozes-Hermitage has also risen: a taste of the best reveals a floral, fruity palate which gains in complexity as it grows older.

Just like other Rhône appellations, though, the vineyards of Crozes vary enormously in terms of *terroir*, ranging from mainly granitic soils in the north, around Gervans, to the clay and limestone slopes of Mercurol further south, which are better suited for white wine production. There is a general consensus (though other vineyard owners would certainly contest it) that the best red Crozes comes from the vines on the plateau that stretches south-to-southeast of Tain-l'Hermitage. Here, the soil is dotted with great stones, similar to the *galets* of Châteauneuf-du-Pape, that soak up the sun and radiate it back to the vines like natural storage heaters. The extra warmth aids ripening and concentrates the grapes – all of which produces an additional elegance in the bottle.

The vineyard area in the Crozes-Hermitage appellation surrounds the vines planted on the hill of Hermitage (above).

MERCUROL
Bernard Chave
Stop here to try some of the best red and white Crozes around, made from just 8ha of vines, as well as a fine red Hermitage.
Domaine la Négociale
Gérard Collonge makes a very accessible Crozes at this estate.
Domaine du Pavillon
A domaine that was once a fruit farm, where the quality-conscious Stephane Cornu works alongside his father to produce some award-winning wines, both red and white.
Domaine des Remizières
Philippe Desmeure uses a long maceration to achieve his generous, full-bodied Crozes.
Domaine St-Jemms
Robert Michelas produces good, balanced Crozes at this estate.

PONT-DE-L'ISERE

Domaine Alain Graillot
Graillot is a perfectionist winegrower producing superior red and white Crozes-Hermitage, as well as a little red Hermitage. Try La Guiraude, the top red Crozes-Hermitage.

Domaine des Grives
A father-and-son operation, where Maurice and Laurent Combier make stylish Crozes (red and white), as well as some St-Joseph. Try the Clos des Grives, named for the ruined petrol station near the entrance to the estate.

WINE FESTIVALS AND FAIRS

● Last weekend in October: wine festival in Crozes-Hermitage.

HOTELS

l'Abricotine
Mercurol
Tel: 4 75 07 44 60
This small, 11-room hotel is not in Mercurol itself but on the D532 towards Chanos-Curson. It stands in a small, walled garden and offers clean, comfortable rooms. The restaurant is exclusively for hotel customers and their guests and is open only in the evening.

Hôtel de la Tour
Mercurol
Tel: 4 75 07 40 07
This simple country hotel in the steep main street has 20 rooms. It also offers a restaurant called La Dauphine.

RESTAURANT

Chabran
Pont-de-l'Isère
Tel: 4 75 84 60 09
Superior restaurant where the cuisine is inventive. Modern tapestries hang in the dining room; you can also eat on the windowed verandah or the garden terrace. Offers an extensive selection of Rhône wines as well as a dozen pleasant hotel rooms.

LOCAL ATTRACTIONS

● A Wednesday market is held in Pont-de-l'Isère.

The northern reaches of Crozes-Hermitage are the appellation's hilliest part, and you could begin your tour of the region here and work your way south. Sadly, though, the villages in this area haven't much to recommend themselves in the way of sights. Serves-sur-Rhône, for example, is some ten kilometres north of Tain-l'Hermitage and most easily reached by the N7. A thriving wine-producing centre during the 18th century, modern Serves makes hardly any wine to speak of. For the most part, it is just a rather grey, main-road community, although entering the town from the north provides a superb view of its impressive castle ruins. What Serves lacks in modern appeal, however, it makes up for in romantic history. Legend has it that in 1248, Louis XII crossed the river here. He and his entourage paused on a flat rock, where they were served Hermitage as well as a number of local specialities. This rock, which can still be seen, has been called *La Table du Roi* ('the king's table') ever since.

Erôme, the next village directly south of Serves, has a bit more to offer in visual terms, including a quaint little square just past the village church which features a curious brick monument and a white statue of a madonna. Further south on the N7 lies the smaller town of Gervans, set on a low hill beside the *route nationale*, and partly surrounded by vineyards which have a similar soil structure and position to some of those in the Hermitage vineyard.

Just past Gervans, there is a turning to Crozes-Hermitage, the village which gave its name to the appellation and was the site of its first *commune*. In the 17th century, wine was the most important source of income here, but today, Crozes seems content to snooze in the shadow of the great hill of Hermitage, a sleepy little village set in a valley beside a small stream. Signs point the way to a couple of view-points in the area; the one marked Pierre-Aiguille is well worth a visit for spectacular views of Tain-l'Hermitage, Tournon, the foothills of Vercor to the east and the Doux Valley to the west. Like Gervans, Crozes is also home to some castle ruins.

From Crozes-Hermitage, the route can be continued east along the D163A to Larnage (more castle ruins, here), across the *autoroute* and then south along the Chantemerle-les-Blés road to Mercurol.

The village of Mercurol is built on a hillside which is dominated by the tower of a ruined 11th-century castle; stop near the little white village church for a fine view. Fruit trees and vineyards abound in Mercurol, and it is generally accepted that the first vines were probably planted here during the 11th century. Another school of thought argues for a much earlier date, though, for the village name could well have been derived from that of the Roman god Mercury; remains of what is thought to have been a Roman temple have been found in the area.

Left *The village of Mercurol, which is known for producing good Crozes-Hermitage – both red and white.*

From Mercurol, follow the D532 east to the wine village of Chanos-Curson, then turn south to Beaumont-Monteux. The village is situated on the River Isère, and has a Romanesque church that is worth a visit.

From there, turn west towards the River Rhône, following signs for Pont-de-l'Isère. You will pass through a flat landscape along the way, with vineyards stretching out over wide plateaux. The journey ends at Pont-de-l'Isère, a village named for a wooden bridge constructed here in 1769. Half a century later, it was replaced by a more permanent stone structure.

Below   Vines flourish near Chanos-Curson. Grapes from these sloping vineyards are often blended with those from flatter terrains to produce wines with greater complexity.

While the bridge at Pont-de-l'Isère connects two sides of a river, the city of Valence, the next destination in our tour of the Rhône and only a short drive south along the N7, acts as a 'bridge' between ancient and modern times.

VALENCE

The city of Valence, often called the 'gateway to Provence, Vercors and Vivarais', was founded by the Romans in the second century BC. Since those days, it has grown into a bustling provincial centre of over 100,000 people, spread over a series of terraces leading down to the River Rhône.

Valence has been a university town since 1452, and its population ebbs and flows with the number of students who come here to study everything from arts to engineering and law. The university was founded by the *dauphin* Louis, later Louis IX. One of the students in its arts faculty was François Rabelais (ca 1494–1553), said to have had a love affair with the daughter of a law professor. Valence is also the place where the young Napoleon Bonaparte completed his military education in 1786, at the school of artillery.

The oldest and most attractive district of Valence lies close to the river. This section of the city is reached either by following the N7 down the river until you reach the Avenue Gambetta, where you will turn left just north of the N532, or by taking the N532 itself across the Rhône from St-Péray. To the right, you will see the Parc Jouvet, a six-hectare oasis of green. Immediately past the park – again to the right – lies the square known as the Champ de Mars, built on a hillside opposite the Rhône, where it is usually easy to park. From here, it is just a few minutes' walk to practically all the interesting sights Valence has to offer. There are also plenty of shops in the area.

HOTELS

Hôtel de Paris et des Voyageurs
30 Avenue Pierre Semard
Tel: 4 75 84 59 40
A centrally located hotel which offers over 36 small but perfectly comfortable rooms, all of which have been double-glazed to cope with the noise from the city streets. There is no restaurant, however.

Park Hôtel
22 Rue Jean-Bouin
Tel: 4 75 43 37 06
The Park is situated in the heart of Valence, and offers around 20 rooms (all with soundproofing). No restaurant.

Below *The city of Valence may not be the quietest place to stay, but it makes an ideal base for touring the villages of the Die Country.*

RESTAURANTS
Le Père Joseph
9 Place des Clercs
Tel: 4 75 42 57 80
This cosy hostelry is situated near
the marketplace, and serves delicious
regional cuisine at exceptionally
reasonable prices. Open every day,
all year round.
Pic
285 Avenue Victor Hugo
Tel: 4 75 44 15 32
For gastronomes – or anyone else
with time to spare – spending two
or three hours in this family-run
restaurant is a worthwhile
experience. Pic boasts Michelin stars,
and the food is not only fantastically
cooked, but it is served in an
exceptionally friendly manner. The
wine list is, frankly, phenomenal, and
the spacious dining room opens onto
a splendid garden. There are also a
few luxurious hotel rooms.
Le St-Ruf
6 Rue Sabaterie
Tel: 4 75 43 48 64
The St-Ruf uses extremely fresh
ingredients as the basis for its cuisine.
Customers also receive a warm
welcome in addition to good food.

The viewpoint on the west side of the Champ de Mars
provides a fine view of the Parc Jouvet, as well as a castle
on the nearby Crussol Mountain. A staircase below the
viewpoint leads to the Avenue Maurice-Faure; turn right
here and head north into the old town centre. The narrow
Rue des Repenties and Côte St-Estève lead around
St-Apollinaire's Cathedral to the Place du Pendentif. The
Pendentif, from which the place takes it name, is a small
funerary monument set to the north of the cathedral.
St-Apollinaire's is Romanesque for the most part, although
the belfry was replaced by a neo-Romanesque tower
sometime during the 19th century.

Walking around the east end of the cathedral leads to the
Place des Ormeaux, where the *Musée des Beaux-Arts*
(Museum of Fine Arts) is located, housed in a former
bishop's palace. There is much to see here – everything
from archaeological finds to contemporary art. Included
among the museum's holdings is a splendid collection of
19th-century pre-Impressionist paintings, as well as abstract
art from the 1950-1970 period, but its main claim to fame
is a huge collection of nearly 100 works by the artist
Hubert Robert (1733-1808). Other attractions include
Gallo-Roman mosaics – depicting themes such as the
labours of Hercules – and a natural history collection. From

Left *The Parc Jouvet, which is overlooked by the Champ de Mars esplanade, provides a welcome respite from the bustle of Valence's city centre.*

the museum, head eastwards until you come to the Grand Rue; turn left and walk northwards until you come to the *Maison des Têtes* – 'The House of Heads'. This Renaissance house (at number 57) owes its name to four enormous heads high up on its façade, each symbolizing one of the four winds. The façade itself is richly decorated in the Flamboyant and Renaissance styles. Behind the *Maison des Têtes* lies a charming courtyard, and it was opposite this house that Napoleon made his residence as a military cadet.

Continue heading north on the Grand Rue, then take the first left and turn right in the Rue du Lieutenant Bonaparte. At number seven you will find the *Maison Dupré-Latour*, which merits attention for a sublime Renaissance stairway located in the courtyard. For the energetic with more time on their hands, a longer walk through the centre of town reveals a number of steep streets and alleyways, including the Côte St-Martin, one of the best-preserved terraced cobbled streets in town.

Valence makes an ideal base from which to take an excursion out of the Rhône region to explore the Drôme Valley to the east. Here, at the base of the Alps, lies the Die Country, a region marked by tiny villages, dramatic mountain backdrops – and, of course, a range of wines.

THE DROME VALLEY

To the east of Valence and the River Rhône lies the Drôme Valley, from which the corresponding *département* takes its name. In addition to the fact that this is a particularly scenic area, the Drôme also falls under the Clairette de Die *appellation contrôlée*, which is the chief reason it has been included in this guide.

The most important town in the area is Die, where wine has been produced since ancient times. In AD77, the Roman historian Pliny the Elder wrote in praise of a sweet wine he considered to be the best in the empire; unusually for the times, it was a wine that could be drunk pure and unadulterated (most others had to be diluted with water, honey, resin or berries just to make them palatable). Pliny knew the wine as *Voconces*, named after the tribe who created it; later, it would be named after the town of Die.

In 1380, a decree was enacted that forbade the importing and use in Die of any but local grapes – and even today, you'll find no Roussanne or Marsanne here. Most Drôme Valley wines are sparkling, made chiefly from a blend of Clairette and Muscat grapes. The latter has probably been here since Roman times, for the variety Pliny described was susceptible to damp and rot, and its very sweet grapes attracted bees – all characteristics that apply exactly to Muscat, which makes up more than half the vineyards in the area.

The term *Clairette de Die* actually refers to wine made by the ancient *méthode dioise ancestrale*, in which the juice is fermented quite slowly at very low temperatures. The wine is then bottled before it has fully matured, and fermentation continues in bottle. The carbon dioxide produced cannot escape, and remains trapped under pressure in the wine, hence its bubbles. Clairette de Die is made from at least

Below *Grapes from vineyards in the Drôme* département, *such as these near Vinsobres, could produce either Côtes du Rhône-Villages or Clairette de Die wines.*

75 per cent Muscat grapes. It has a fruity aroma, tastes both fresh and slightly sweet, and, at 7.5 per cent, is relatively low in alcohol. It is also wholly natural, for nothing is added. The other type of sparkling wine is made exclusively from Clairette grapes and uses the *méthode champenoise*; in other words, it undergoes secondary fermentation in bottle, stimulated by adding some sugar and yeast cells to the wine. Although it can still be known as *Clairette de Die Brut*, its official name is now *Crémant de Die*.

Still wines are also made in Die Country. There is Coteaux de Die, made solely from Clairette grapes; and Châtillon-en-Diois, which is mainly red and made chiefly from Gamay, although Syrah and Pinot Noir can be used. Some rosé is also produced, as well as some white wine made from Aligoté and Chardonnay. Whatever their colour, however, the still wines are usually of a lesser quality than their sparkling cousins. In this valley of the effervescent Drôme, sparkling wines are a fitting speciality.

In contrast to the River Rhône, where bridge-building, canalisation and other kinds of work have been carried out along most of its length, the Drôme, which flows into the Rhône about halfway between Valence and Montélimar, is relatively untamed. The surrounding landscape is also distinctly different, being very hilly – even mountainous – in some places. The vegetation takes elements from Provence and the nearby Alps; thus, there are more camping sites here than industrial ones. Most of the towns and villages are relatively small and very ancient, a fact which adds to the enjoyment of the drive east from Crest. Around every bend, you will see another view of far-off mountains and nearby woodlands, meadows, orchards, lavender fields and vineyards, and down below the silver ribbon of the river and its stony bed.

Above A dramatic landscape surrounds the town of Die, which lies at the heart of the Clairette de Die wine district.

RECOMMENDED PRODUCERS

AUREL

Domaine des Muttes
Raymond Bec and his sons work
15ha in Aurel, which is around 6km
from Vercheny, producing a Clairette
with a good deal of finesse.

Georges Raspail
Raspail is known throughout the
region for his sparkling Muscat wine.

BARSAC

Claude Achard
Achard is considered one of the
leading growers of Clairette de Die.

Domaine des Adrets
This estate belongs to the Maillefaud
family, who make traditional, Muscat-
based sparkling wine.

Patrick Lantheaume
A small estate which has only been
in existence since 1988.

Domaine de Magord
Belongs to the winegrower
Jean-Claude Vincent.

Pierre Salabelle
Stop here for very pleasant wine.

THE DIE COUNTRY

There are various ways of getting to the Drôme Valley and
the Die wine district. The quickest route from Valence is
via the D111, which leads directly to Crest. If time is not of
the essence, however, you could turn off in Montoison,
about 12 kilometres south of Valence, and head east towards
Upie on the D342. About midway between the two towns
is *Le Jardin aux Oiseaux* (the Garden of the Birds), open 365
days a year. This park is home to 1,000 birds, including
parrots, flamingos, pelicans, eagles, pheasants, storks and
ostriches. Altogether, around 200 different species are
represented, including the delicate and fascinating hum-
mingbirds, which reside in a special Hummingbird House.
There is also a children's farm at *Le Jardin*, and a restaurant
is open during the summer season.

If feathers are not your forté, then drive southwest from
Montoison along the D125 to Allex, where a tropical
aquarium is situated near the *hôtel de ville,* or town hall. The
aquarium boasts fish and turtles from four continents and
their surrounding seas, including some rare specimens such
as the multi-coloured Mexican cychlasoma and some men-
acing piranha. Whether you choose fish or fowl, Crest is
only about ten kilometres away from either Upie or Allex.

Left and far left *Following the River Drôme as it winds its way eastward reveals a vastly different countryside to that which surrounds the Rhône. Ancient villages seem to grow out of the riverbank or cliff faces, and the rolling hills and mountains give the area an almost Alpine feel.*

The little town of Crest is situated where the River Drôme flows into the Valence plain. It was founded in the tenth century by the Arnaud family, who named it *Crista Arnaudarum*. The Crest skyline is dominated by an imposing keep – at 51 metres, the tallest in France – all that is left of a massive, hillside fortress that was dismantled in 1632 on the orders of Louis XIII. Built in various stages between the 12th and 15th centuries, its foundations are much older, dating from Roman times. During the religious wars, the keep was occupied in turn by both Protestants and Catholics, and often served as a prison. The last prisoners held here were 600 Republican opponents of Louis Napoleon's *coup* of 1851. One of its great rooms contains a collection of old weapons. It is well worth the effort of climbing the steps to the top terrace, where there is a spectacular view over the rooftops of Crest to the surrounding countryside.

After descending from the keep to the bottom of the Rue de la Tour, turn right and follow the hilltop path that runs around the east end of an old Franciscan church. Nearby, further down the hill to the left, is *Le Portique* – the Franciscans' Portico – a covered passageway which leads to the Franciscans' Steps. This is an amazing stairway with 124 steps, most of them cut into solid rock.

DIE
Buffardel Frères
One of the smaller wine businesses in Die.
Cave Coopérative Clairette de Die
By far the largest producer in the area. Despite its considerable volume, however, both sparkling and still wines are of a high average quality. The co-op supplies the entire range of wines from this valley, including Domaine de Blanchon, a *vin de pays* made from Chardonnay. An excellent Coteaux de Die bears the name Domaine des Tours. Various brand names are used for the sparkling wines.

PONTAIX
Patrick Marcel
In production since 1983, Marcel's estate lies on the Pontaix to Barsac road.
Alain Poulet
Try some of Poulet's sparkling Muscat.

SAILLANS
Jean-Claude Raspail
This Raspail operates a tasting centre on the D93. His Crémant de Die, Clairette de Die and the still Coteaux de Die are all of high quality.

ST-ROMAN
Didier Cornillon/ Clos de Beylière
The most important private producer of Châtillon-en-Diois (St-Roman is 3.5km from Châtillon). This winegrower has vines in Châtillon that are half a century old and grow at 600m above sea level. Besides still wines (the red Châtillon-en-Diois is delicious), Cornillon makes a prize-winning Crémant de Die.

STE-CROIX
Archard-Vincent
Located in Ste-Croix, which lies between Pontaix and Die, this estate is known as one of the prominent producers of quality Clairette de Die.

VERCHENY
Carod Frères
The Carod family has been making wine for several generations. The attractive *Musée de la Clairette* (Museum of Clairette) has been established on the estate.
Jacques Faure
Try both the Clairette de Die and Crémant de Die.
Monge-Granon
This large wine estate of roughly 30ha was established in 1985.
Union des Jeunes Viticulteurs Récoltants (UJVR)
The Union is made up of about 10 young winegrowers, who together work some 60ha. They produce Crémant de Die, Clairette de Die and Coteaux de Die under the Chamberan label.

Below *Lavender fields form close neighbours to vineyards in the countryside near Châtillon-en-Diois.* Far right *Dominated as it is by its austere, imposing keep, the skyline of Crest is unmistakable.*

The centre of Crest consists of just a few streets and some alleyways, but it is well worth a quiet stroll through the Rue de la République, the main street. As well as its shops and art specialists, there are a number of Renaissance buildings, including vast 16th- and 17th-century mansions which once belonged to the village's wealthier *bourgeoisie*. Crest also has a natural history museum, the *Musée de la Nature*, which contains minerals and precious stones as well as the requisite dinosaur bones.

You should also try to have a meal in the village, for Crest offers several local specialities, including *picodons*, delicious, small goat's cheeses.

Leave Crest by means of the D93 – a very good road nowadays. The valley gets ever more beautiful the further along you travel, and at Saillans the vineyards appear. Turn off to the left on the D493 to visit this village. From the narrow main thoroughfare, a street leads at right angles to the *hôtel de ville* (town hall), which is situated on slightly higher ground. Here, and in the nearby Romanesque church, a number of Roman boundary stones have been assembled. To the side of the *hôtel de ville* is a shady court, redolent with atmosphere, where locals play *jeu de boules*. A visit to Saillans can be concluded with some wine-tasting beside the D93 at the premises of Jean-Claude Raspail, one of the district's most energetic growers.

Back on the D93, the next village you'll come to is Vercheny, a typical holiday resort complete with camp-sites, canoes for hire, and various places for wine-tasting. Here, you could cross the Drôme and follow the D157 and D739 to Barsac – not the town of Sauternes fame, but an isolated hamlet which does produce good wine of its own. The vineyards here are surrounded by rugged mountains, which also shelter them from rough weather.

Continue your journey along the D93 to Pontaix, a small village nestled below a cliff and a ruined castle. Be prepared for some dramatic scenery just past the town: 1,000-metre rock faces rise to the right of the road, while down below to the left, the River Drôme winds through its valley, set about with groves of trees, vineyards and a few scattered farms. A few kilometres further on, the landscape opens out and the town of Die comes into view, set against a backdrop of brown and blue-grey mountains.

Die is the centre of the wine district – a fact made clear by the presence of what is by far the area's largest producer, the *cave coopérative*, which is situated on the Avenue de la Clairette, the main road into town.

WINE-RELATED ATTRACTIONS
- Signposts mark out a route around the cellars of this wine district.
- In Upie, Jean Sorrel produces his own distilled drinks from fruits of the region.

HOTELS
Grand Hôtel
Crest
Tel: 4 75 25 08 17
Not the best choice for people with a lot of luggage, the Grand is situated in the main street and you cannot park in front of the entrance. Still, there are about 20 comfortable rooms, and the Grand has its own restaurant where you eat quite well and inexpensively.

Hôtel Xavier-Gras
Saillans
Tel: 4 75 21 51 10
Located in the now-quiet main street, the Xavier-Gras offers simple rooms, and a restaurant where regional dishes are served.

La Petite Auberge
Die
Tel: 4 75 22 05 91
On the same road as the Relais (below), but further into town, the Auberge offers 11 pleasant, simple rooms. There is also a good restaurant which offers an agreeable set menu.

Relais de Chamarges
Die
Tel: 4 75 22 00 95
This is the only hotel in Die situated just outside the town, almost opposite the wine *coopérative*. It has 9 rooms; numbers 6 to 9 are at the rear, with a fine view. Although they are fairly small, the rooms are all comfortable and clean. Sometimes you can hear the noise from the bar below. Simple country dishes are served in the rustic-style restaurant.

St-Domingue
Die
Tel: 4 75 22 03 08
This is the most comfortable hotel in the main street. It has 26 good-sized rooms with traditional furnishings, a swimming pool and a small garage. There is also a good restaurant.

RESTAURANTS
Kléber
Crest
Tel: 4 75 25 11 69
The furnishings of this restaurant are perhaps more modern than the cuisine, but the dishes – regional and Provençal – are carefully and deliciously prepared. Try the set lunch menu on weekdays. Guests can also be accommodated in 7 rooms.

La Porte Montségur
Crest
Tel: 4 75 25 41 48
Located on the eastern side of Crest, the Montségur offers regional cuisine in season, which you can choose to eat out on the terrace in fine weather. There are also around 9 modern hotel rooms.

Rive Gauche
Crest
Tel: 4 75 25 50 61
This small, stylish establishment could well develop into the best in Crest, thanks to an inventive chef who produces delicious, innovative dishes.

Patrick Giffon
Grane
Tel: 4 75 62 60 64
Less than 10km from Crest. You'll receive warm hospitality in the Giffon, which serves both classic and more contemporary dishes, all skilfully prepared. Situated near the town church, the restaurant also has 11 somewhat noisy hotel rooms, and a swimming pool.

Le Rieussec
Saillans
Tel: 4 75 21 56 43
A popular and modern concern, with bar, situated on a road parallel to the D93 and offering simple country food and low prices. The owners come from Burgundy, and their origins are evident in some of the dishes.

Le Moulin
Châtillon-en-Diois
Tel: 4 75 21 10 73
A very agreeable place where they cook with dedication. Everything is prepared on the premises, including the *terrine de foie gras*. Specialities include sweetbreads and *ravioli de langoustines à la Clairette*. Le Moulin also stocks delicious wines from Didier Cornillon. Open May to mid-October.

LOCAL ATTRACTIONS

● Tuesdays, Wednesdays, Fridays and Saturdays: market in Crest.
● August: festival of vocal jazz in Crest.
● Thematic exhibitions, changed annually, are held in the castle keep at Crest.
● Sunday: market in Saillans.
● Wednesday and Saturday: market day in Die.
● Friday: market day in Châtillon-en-Diois.

In Roman times, when the valley was inhabited by the Celtic Voconces, the town was known as *Dea Augusta*. Well-to-do Roman merchants had houses and estates here, as is shown by displays in the local museum. Unlike many towns in the Rhône Valley, however, few external monuments remain from that time; when the Roman empire collapsed, the people of Die transformed all available stones into walls to defend the town from barbarian attacks. Here and there in the remains of these walls you can still see stones bearing Roman inscriptions.

The town does boast one Roman monument, the Porte St-Marcel, which dates from the first half of the third century. It can be found close to the most important building in Die, the imposing white cathedral of Notre-Dame. Although built in the 12th century (as can be seen from the Romanesque west door) the cathedral was largely destroyed by the Huguenots during the 17th century, and later rebuilt in its present form. Austere as it is, Notre-Dame is surrounded by a delightful tree-filled square. Nearby in the episcopal chapel – which now belongs to the *hôtel de ville* (town hall) – you can find a magnificent mosaic depicting an earthly paradise, which dates from the 12th century but is Gallo-Roman in style.

From Die, you could take a trip out to Châtillon-en-Diois – take the D93, then turn left on the D539. Halfway there, near the junction of the D93 and the D120, you will

see the remains of the castle of Aix-en-Diois, with a few ruined walls and a round tower. As mentioned on page 73, Châtillon has given its name to a small wine district. Unlike most wine villages in the area, the local church is Protestant.

Return to Crest and follow the D104 until it runs into the N7, where you will head south towards Montélimar, the next stage in our journey.

Above *Caught between rock and water, the village of Pontaix clings firmly to its cliff face.*

Left *Die, surrounded by mountain mists. As long ago as 77AD, wines made in Die were praised for their natural sweetness.*

The Southeastern Rhône

In the Rhône Valley, around 60 per cent of all wine bearing an *appellation contrôlée* consists of Côtes du Rhône, while the superior Côtes du Rhône-Villages represents a further five to ten per cent. While the appellation itself actually takes in six *départements* – the Ardèche, the Drôme, the Gard, the Loire, the Rhône and the Vaucluse – the bulk of these wines is produced in the southeastern part of the Rhône region, which stretches out from the river itself to mountain ranges such as the Dentelles du Montmirail. The huge Côtes du Rhône appellation, which in 1995 amounted to 44,735 hectares and whose crop (in volume terms) only just falls short of Bordeaux, includes more than 100 *communes* north of Avignon. Many villages in this area are built on hills and used to be fortified, but between them stretch wide plateaux full of vines. Vineyards also flourish on the hilly slopes, particularly in the *communes* that produce Côtes du Rhône-Villages, which has an official vineyard of roughly 3,662 hectares.

Planting in the southeastern Rhône increased on a great scale after the Second World War, and thanks to better techniques, the yield per hectare has improved significantly. Cooperatives have played quite a dominant role, here: an estimated 70 per cent of all Côtes du Rhône is made by this type of concern. There are even *communes* in which the *cave coopérative* vinifies all, or nearly all, of the wine. These co-op wines can often be of a high quality; this is certainly true of the special *cuvées* which nearly every establishment offers nowadays. Wines of this type are made from selected grapes, and they often spend time in cask. But be warned: not all Villages wines are equally attractive or interesting, so a careful choice has been made for this guide.

Left Vinsobres is just one of the 16 villages in the Rhône entitled to use its name on Côtes du Rhône-Villages wine. Rasteau's vignobles (above) might do the same – but they might also make vin doux naturel.

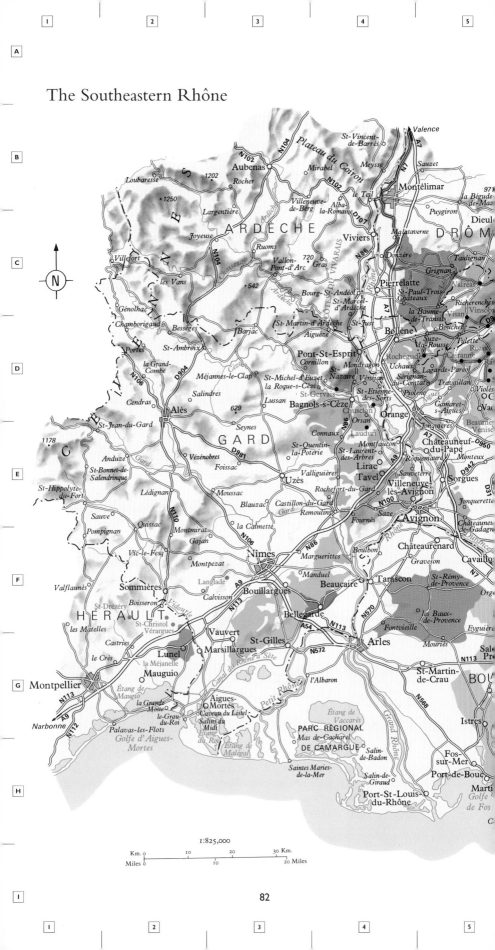

The Southeastern Rhône

▢	Châteauneuf-du-Pape
▢	Gigondas
▢	Vacqueyras
▢	Tavel
▢	Lirac
▢	Rasteau
▢	Muscat de Beaumes-de-Venise
▢	Coteaux du Tricastin
▢	Côtes du Ventoux
▢	Clairette de Bellegarde
▢	Muscat de Lunel
▢	Côtes du Rhône/-Villages
▢	Côtes du Lubéron
▢	Costières de Nîmes
▢	Coteaux d'Aix-en-Provence
▢	Les Baux-de-Provence

–·–·–·	Département boundary
Rochegude	Côtes du Rhône-Villages
● Langlade	Coteaux du Languedoc commune
CÔTES DU VIVARAIS	VDQS
▭	Wine route

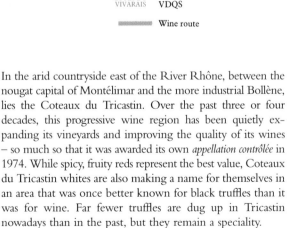

In the arid countryside east of the River Rhône, between the nougat capital of Montélimar and the more industrial Bollène, lies the Coteaux du Tricastin. Over the past three or four decades, this progressive wine region has been quietly expanding its vineyards and improving the quality of its wines – so much so that it was awarded its own *appellation contrôlée* in 1974. While spicy, fruity reds represent the best value, Coteaux du Tricastin whites are also making a name for themselves in an area that was once better known for black truffles than it was for wine. Far fewer truffles are dug up in Tricastin nowadays than in the past, but they remain a speciality.

The route through the southeastern Rhône begins at Montélimar, carries on through the Coteaux du Tricastin and then tours through over 20 villages of the Côtes du Rhône, ending in the historic town of Vaison-la-Romaine. Then, later on in the guide, it is the turn of the villages of the southern Rhône.

Right *Almond trees bloom near Montélimar, ensuring a steady supply of the basic ingredient for the city's thriving nougat industry.*

MONTELIMAR

Anyone driving into the town of Montélimar will soon be aware that nougat is the local speciality. Everywhere, signs in shops and small factories extol the virtues of this sticky confection. Almonds are one main ingredient; sugar, honey and egg whites are the others. Nougat was most probably first made in Marseille, but only after the first almond trees had been planted in France during the 16th century.

By the 17th century, once almond-growing had been established right across the Gras Plateau, nougat-making flourished in Montélimar, due to its location as well as to the abundant supply of honey available from neighbouring Provence. The confectionery business quickly became a mainstay of the town, and handmade Montélimar nougat gained an excellent reputation throughout Europe. Factory production began in the 20th century, and the business expanded even further – as is evident from the confectionery shops scattered along the Allées du Champ-de-Mars.

Of course, Montélimar has more than nougat to offer. Like most cities in the Rhône, the town's roots go back to the Romans, who knew it as *Accusium*. The present name derives from *Montilium Adhémari*, or 'Mont Adhémar', the name of a mighty hill-top castle built and fortified in the early Middle Ages by the powerful Adhémar family, and subsequently enlarged during the following centuries. The castle, which is situated east of the town, served primarily as a prison until the 1930s, but today its main apartments function as a museum and are open to the public. If you fancy a terrific view west over the town and east towards the Drôme, visit the imposing Narbonne Tower on the castle's north side and climb the spiral staircase to the parapet. The castle keep has nine beautiful Romanesque windows, and there are some 12th-century frescoes located in the chapel.

Sadly, Montélimar suffered severe war damage during the Second World War, which resulted in the loss of much of its original architecture. However, the 15th-century Ste-Croix Collegiate Church still stands in the centre of the old town, surrounded by ancient streets with overhanging eaves. Montélimar also makes a good base from which to tour the Coteaux du Tricastin.

MONTELIMAR

HOTELS

Relais de l'Empereur
1 Place Marx-Dormony
Tel: 4 75 01 29 00
This stylish, classic hotel is situated in the middle of the city and features a terraced garden in addition to its 30 rooms. The restaurant serves primarily traditional cuisine.

Le Sphinx
22 Rue Jean-Bouin
Tel: 4 75 01 96 64
The Sphinx is a 17th-century building which boasts around 2 dozen spacious rooms that have been furnished with antiques. Friendly service adds to its charms.

RESTAURANT

La Petite France
34 Impasse Raymond-Daujat
Tel: 4 75 46 07 94
Inventive dishes are served alongside more traditional cuisine in this reliable restaurant.

THE COTEAUX DU TRICASTIN

The 22 *communes* that make up the Coteaux du Tricastin lie south and southeast of Montélimar; all belong to the Drôme *département*. The name *Tricastin* comes from an ancient Celtic people known as the *Tricastini*, a warlike tribe who lived here during pre-Roman times.

During the first half of the 20th century, the region was better known for its black truffles than for its wine – which is the reason it was not included in the Côtes du Rhône appellation. In the 1960s, however, winegrowing got under way again, and today the vineyard of the Coteaux du Tricastin contains about 2,400 hectares of vines. These are spread about a dry, windswept landscape that is interspersed with olive groves and cypress trees, but improvements in vineyard techniques have nonetheless made the Coteaux an up-and-coming region. More reds than whites are produced here, and many bear a strong resemblance to Côtes du Rhône. The best and most aromatic wines contain a considerable proportion of Syrah, or are even made exclusively from this grape; best drunk young, they tend to be spicy and fruity, and represent very good value. While the best of the whites can be fresh and full-flavoured, they are not generally as exciting as the reds. Some rosé is also made, but many of these have an alcohol content that is just slightly too high to be enjoyable.

This part of the southeastern Rhône offers a great deal to see for the wine tourist, therefore the suggested route starts at Montélimar and continues through the most interesting of the Coteaux du Tricastin *communes*.

Head south from Montélimar on the N7. The first village in the Coteaux du Tricastin appellation is Malataverne, about nine kilometres from Montélimar. Turn right towards the village, where, on the south side, you will find a road leading up to the chapel of Notre-Dame de Montchamp, where there is a burial site from Merovingian times as well as a fine view of the surrounding area.

RECOMMENDED PRODUCERS

LA BAUME-DE-TRANSIT
Domaine du Bois Noir
Jean-Pierre Estève makes good Côtes du Rhône alongside his Coteaux du Tricastin wines.
Domaine St-Guery
Owner Guy Renaud makes a reliable red that is matured in wood.
Domaine St-Luc
This estate, run by Loduvic Cornillon, is one of the very best in the Coteaux du Tricastin. Be sure to taste his 100% Syrah, as well as the easy-drinking white.

BOLLENE
Château la Croix Chabrière
A real château, where the ground-level cellar looks almost like a temple. The wine estate lies along the road from St-Restitut to Bollène, and it is here that owner Patrick Daniel makes good red, rosé and white wines.

LES GRANGES-GONTARDES
Domaine de la Tour d'Elyssas
This domaine can be relied upon for consistently good wines.
Domaine du Vieux Micocoulier
Stop here and try the excellent red Coteaux du Tricastin. This extensive wine estate is run enthusiastically by Jean and Georges Vergobbi.

Below The medieval hilltop village of La Garde-Adhémar is considered one of the most beautiful in the entire Coteaux du Tricastin.

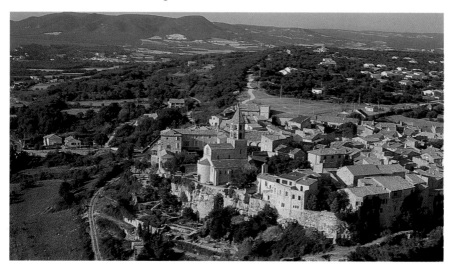

GRIGNAN
Domaine de Montine
This estate, run by Jean-Luc
Monteillet, is recommended for its
red, rosé and white Coteaux du
Tricastin; the red shows a mixture of
truffles and jam on the palate.

ROUSSAS
Domaine de Grangeneuve
At this exceptionally reliable estate,
the Bour family produces glorious
red wines. The best of them are
wholly, (or mostly) Syrah, but
Grenache and Cinsaut are also
used. These are deeply coloured
reds, with fine aromas and well-
balanced palates – very easy to drink.

ST-PAUL-TROIS-CHATEAUX
Château la Décelle
The Séroin family makes delicious
red wines and an exciting rosé at
this estate.

VALAURIE
Domaine du Serre Rouge
The Blanchet family produces
special *cuvées* with a large
Syrah content.

WINE-RELATED FACTS
● Coteaux du Tricastin is also
produced by a number of
cooperatives within the Côtes
du Rhône area, such as those
at Suze-la-Rousse and Rochegude.

Below *The village of Roussas rises
aboves its vineyards. Despite its size,
it is one of the main wine-producing
villages in the Coteaux du Tricastin.*

Continue heading south on the N7 for around seven
kilometres before turning right to the village of Donzère.
Don't be put off by the industrial works around the river;
head instead into the old, partly medieval centre of the
village and visit the church of St-Philibert, which was built
in Romanesque/Byzantine style. Donzère also has an
archaeological museum, but if you prefer outdoor pursuits,
then now is the time to head towards the River Rhône on
the D486 for a view of the impressive Défilé de Donzère.
This beautiful canyon is traditionally considered to be the
real gateway to Provence – a much more attractive
description than it held previously, when bargemen
considered it one of the most treacherous parts of the river.

Once back in Donzère, take the D541 south (in the
direction of Bollène), and continue on it eastwards to Les
Granges-Gontardes. The scenery which surrounds this little
village is much more rural, and the atmosphere more
peaceful. Even so, Les Granges-Gontardes has its own share
of culture to offer, in the form of the local museum which
boasts a collection of pottery that is renowned among
archaeologists the world over.

Continue heading east on the D541 to Valaurie. A
number of craftsmen and artists are established in this
village, which has undergone extensive restoration since the
mid-1960s. If you happen to be touring the area in
December, then be sure to visit the annual Salon d'Artisanat
et des Produits Gourmands.

The neighbouring village of Roussas is the next
destination. Situated southwest of Valaurie and reached by
the D553, it stands on a hill surrounded by vineyards and is
dominated by a partially occupied castle. The keep can be
climbed and rewards the effort with a complete panorama
of the surrounding countryside. Roussas also has an ancient
chapel, set high above the town.

If you are more interested in churches on a grand scale,
then leave Roussas via the D203 and head northeast to the
abbey of Notre-Dame de Aiguebelle (the D203 runs into
the D550, where the abbey is located). Founded by the
Cistercians in the 12th century, the abbey was expropriated
during the French Revolution, but the monks managed to
buy it back in 1815. The main building was almost in ruins
by then, and haş been subsequently restored, but the
cloisters are original and border on a flower garden. The
monks who reside here follow a strict vegetarian diet, but –
this being France, after all – they do get wine to drink.
They also make various syrups and two good liqueurs (a
green and a slightly sweeter yellow version; both are called
Aiguebelle, or sometimes *Liqueur de Frère Jean*) made from
various herbs, roots, flowers and seeds.

Follow the D550 southwest from the abbey until you
come to a crossroads; then turn left on the D56 to the
village of Réauville. Here you can either visit the remains
of an 11th-century tower, or – for the gourmetically
minded – call in at Le Caveur, a firm where truffle producer

André Feraud sells directly to private customers. From Réauville, continue east on the D56, either all the way to the tiny village of Salles-sous-Bois, a little to the north, which boasts some fine old buildings, or else turning south on the D4 and heading straight to Grignan.

This village has been a place of pilgrimage for many literature students, ever since the letters of the 17th-century Marquise de Sévigné (1626-1696), 'the greatest letter-writer in Europe', were collected and published. Look above the rooftops of Grignan and you will see the massive château where the marquise's daughter (and later the marquise herself) lived after marrying the Comte de Grignan, the king's lieutenant-governor in Provence and the last scion of the Adhémar family of Montélimar fame. The wonderful descriptions of 17th-century court life that Madame de Sévigné is remembered for were conveyed in 1,500 letters written to her daughter over 30 years. She died in the château – 'a fine and magnificent' place, in her own words – on April 17, 1696, not quite 70 years old.

The château itself suffered extensive damage during the French Revolution, but fortunately it was saved from complete destruction by the wealthy lawyer, Léopold Faure, who bought it in 1838. In 1912, comprehensive restoration was carried out by another owner, Madame Fontaine, whose descendants still live there. Today, the château at Grignan is a fine, elegantly decorated Renaissance mansion which commands a wonderful view of Mont Ventoux from its terrace. The adjoining *Musée Faure-Chabrol* was founded by a daughter of Léopold Faure and contains displays of old furniture, 17th-century tapestries – and, of course, mementoes of Madame de Sévigné.

Above The Château la Croix Chabrière estate, near Bollène, produces both Côtes du Rhône and Coteaux du Tricastin wines.

HOTELS
Auberge des Quatre Saisons
St-Restitut
Tel: 4 75 04 71 88
Ten comfortable, tastefully appointed rooms have been established in the group of historic buildings that makes up the Four Seasons.
L'Esplan
St-Paul-Trois-Châteaux
Tel: 4 75 96 64 64
This remarkable hotel comprises 36 rooms with contemporary furnishings – each one different from the others. It has its own large terrace where a gigantic chess game stands. The restaurant places an emphasis on regional cuisine – so truffles are on the menu in season.
La Ferme St-Michel
Solérieux
Tel: 4 75 98 10 66
Located between La Baume-de-Transit and Solérieux, this is a peaceful place to stay, with 15 comfortable, reasonably modern rooms spread over various wings of a 16th-century farmhouse. There is also a swimming pool, tennis court, park and large terrace. Regional dishes – including truffles from the grounds – are served in the vaulted, stylishly furnished dining room.

Right *Grignan, with its impressive château, was once home to lady of letters Madame de Sévigné. Today, it plays host to hundreds of roses.*

Manoir de la Roseraie
Grignan
Tel: 4 75 46 58 15
A country house surrounded by a park and rosebeds, with 15 pleasant, bright rooms. Good restaurant, too.
Sévigné
Grignan
Tel: 4 75 46 50 97
Although the Sévigné features 15 very comfortable rooms, it is unfortunately situated on a bypass by a junction, and doesn't make for a particularly peaceful stay. No restaurant.
La Table de Nicole
Valaurie
Tel: 4 75 98 52 03
This hotel offers 10 good-sized, comfortable rooms which have been kitted out in regional style. You can also eat well in the hotel restaurant, particularly from the *à la carte* menu which offers an extensive choice. Truffles are, of course, included in season.

 RESTAURANTS

Les Buisses
St-Restitut
Tel: 4 75 04 96 50
This country inn actually consists of a Provençal farm with a terrace. It offers generous servings of regional fare, complete with truffles in season.
La Chapelle
St-Paul-Trois-Châteaux
Tel: 4 75 96 60 88
La Chapelle's young owner-chef cooks with pleasure and talent. Fresh fish is often on the menu, and so are seasonal, regional dishes.
L'Eau à la Bouche
Grignan
Tel: 4 75 46 57 37
A good place to try for refined dishes or a juicy *entrecôte*. The restaurant offers a friendly reception, a warm, rustic atmosphere and a terrace.
Le Prédaïou
La Garde-Adhémar
Tel: 4 75 04 40 08
A simple restaurant in an old building, specialising in regional fare, such as *magret de canard au miel*. *Côte de boeuf* is grilled to order.

Among the other attractions at Grignan are the church of St-Sauveur, which features Madame de Sévigné's tombstone as well as some skilful woodcarvings in the choir. There is also a belfry in the old village centre (it was actually built in the 11th century as a gate, and the clock was not added until the 1600s). Sights situated on the western side of Grignan include the Romanesque chapel of St-Vincent and a statue of the marquise. And then there are the roses. Around 150 different types of roses have been planted throughout the village, and a signposted 'rose walk' leads past the best of them.

From Grignan, head southeast on the D941 towards Valréas. On the way, you might visit the *Village Provençal Miniature*, a covered miniature village, and its adjacent shops which offer craft wares, wines and other items (there is also a restaurant if you're feeling peckish).

Turn right off the D941, first onto the D64 and then left onto the D231 to the tiny hamlet of Colonzelle, and visit the chapel of St-Pierre, which was built in Carolingian times and contains a *bas-relief* of Gallo-Roman wine motifs. Then, continue south on the D231 until you come to a T-junction and turn right towards Montségur-sur-Lauzon.

Montségur is a wine village that boasts a Romanesque church and some interesting castle ruins. It also features a strange monument known as the *grand mur gaulois* ('the great wall of Gaul'), which amounts to a section of the town wall on the southeast side of the village that has been dedicated to French dialects. Rumour has it that François Mitterand owned a wood of truffle oaks not far from town.

Leave Montségur and head south on the D117 to La Baume-de-Transit, the next destination. A popular theory states that the latter part of the village name is a corruption of *Tricastin*. Diane de Poitiers, Henri II's mistress, bore the title of *Dame de La Baume-de-Transit*, and to please her, the monarch instituted two fairs here. The village is quite a scenic place, with some interesting old houses, the remains of a castle (with keep) and an early medieval church complete with an open belfry.

From La Baume-de-Transit, take the D341 and D218 west to St-Restitut, an attractive little village with a long history. It acquired its present name from a fifth-century bishop, later canonised, who was born blind but miraculously had his sight restored – an event, or 'restitution' that gave him the name of *Restitut* from then on. The saint is said to be buried under the square tower of the village church. The church itself was constructed in the Provençal Romanesque style, and is worth seeing for its beautifully decorative carvings. Traditionally a place of pilgrimage for the blind, it still attracts people hoping for a miracle cure on November 7, St Restitut's Day. The village is also the home of the 13th-century Maison de la Tour, which used to be the residence of the bishops from nearby St-Paul-Trois-Châteaux. It is a distinguished building that now serves as a cultural centre.

A quarter of an hour's hillside walk north of St-Restitut will bring you to the 16th-century chapel of St-Sépulcre. The *caves cathédrales* are located a few kilometres further on (but you would be advised to take the car to visit them).

Valle Aurea
Valaurie
Tel: 4 75 97 25 00
Stop here for a taste of Provence: delicious, subtle dishes are prepared by a female chef, and served in a convivial dining room. There are also 5 quiet, tastefully decorated hotel rooms, as well as a terrace.

La Vielle France
St-Paul-Trois-Châteaux
Tel: 4 75 96 70 47
The France has been here since the beginning of the 1990s, and has gained a loyal clientele by serving honest cooking and good wines at reasonable prices.

LOCAL ATTRACTIONS

● The black truffles of Tricastin have their own *appellation contrôlée*, defining an area that consists of 68 communes in the Drôme *département* and 15 in the Vaucluse.
● Second Sunday in February: *Fête de la Truffe* in St-Paul-Trois-Châteaux, with tastings, truffle omelettes, etc.
● Saturday is market day in Donzère, as is Wednesday in Les Granges-Gontardes.
● Grignan has a *Centre Vivant de l'Art Contemporain*, with exhibitions of arts and photography.

Below *The peaceful village of Les Granges-Gontardes has a renowned pottery collection to offer, as well as acres of vineyards.*

While it never had three castles, St-Paul-Trois-Châteaux does feature a rather impressive cathedral (above).

- Tuesday is market day in Grignan and in St-Paul-Trois-Châteaux.
- There is a nine-hole golf course called Golf de la Provençale near Clansayes.
- May l: craft fair in St-Restitut.
- Last week of July: three-day village festival in Grignan.
- Beginning of July: honey festival in La Garde-Adhémar.
- Friday is market day in Chamaret.
- During the tourist season, a visual presentation of the history of the Coteaux du Tricastin is given in the Chapelle des Pénitents, by the church square in La Garde-Adhémar. English or German commentary is available.

These immense cellars were once stone quarries; today, they are used by the firm of Celliers des Dauphins to mature some of its wines. Visitors to the *caves* are driven around a tour that lasts about 45 minutes. Besides the wine casks, the *caves* also house an 18th-century press and representations of wine themes with wax figures. A special *tastevin*, or wine-tasting cup, is included in the admission price, and this comes in handy at the end of the tour, when a wine tasting is held. Outside the *caves*, you can enjoy a splendid view of the surrounding countryside.

Follow the D59A to the D59, and head west to St-Paul-Trois-Châteaux, the town that lies at the heart of the chief truffle region of France. The Romans, who knew the town as *Augusta Tricastinorum*, made it capital of the region; in the fourth century, *Augusta* was replaced by *Paul* in honour of one of the town's first bishops. 'Trois Châteaux' is probably a corruption of 'Tricastin', for St-Paul has certainly never had three castles – although it is ringed by walls and gates.

The centre of the village, which is situated on a low hillside, consists of narrow streets full of atmosphere. Sights include the imposing, austere-looking cathedral of St-Paul, another example of Provençal Romanesque architecture that dates from the 11th and 12th centuries. The interior of the cathedral has many interesting features, including the high, barrel-vaulted nave, and some medieval frescoes; there is also an early medieval mosaic behind the gilt high altar which depicts Jerusalem at the time of the crusades.

The *office du tourisme* is situated near the cathedral, and the quaintly named *Maison de la Truffe et du Tricastin* ('The House of the Truffle and Tricastin') has been opened next door. Here, half-a-dozen rooms display all aspects of 'the black diamond' and its impact on the area; the cellars beneath house wines from all over the Tricastin area, as well as exhibits of old winemaking implements.

The village is as popular with sportsmen as it is with gourmets, for it is also home to St-Paul 2003, a large, modern leisure centre complete with bowls, tennis and squash courts, a mini-golf course, swimming pools and other activities. More sedate visitors will be content to stroll through the streets of St-Paul, where they can admire the local architecture, including the 17th-century *hôtel de ville* (town hall) which has a fine façade.

Leave St-Paul-Trois-Châteaux and head northeast on the the D133. After about five kilometres, turn right onto the D571 towards Clansayes, a pleasant village set on a hill. The square tower that rises above the village is known as the *Tour des Templiers*, or 'Tower of the Templars'; in the past, it served as a prison. Clansayes is also home to the chapel of Notre-Dame de Torone, with its cloisters, and the large Fontaine de Jouvence. Many fossils have been found near this village, as well as Stone Age spearheads, axes, and other weapons and tools. You can get a fine view over modern Clansayes from the far end of the promontory, by the huge statue of the Virgin Mary.

The view to the northwest includes La Garde-Adhémar, a medieval village also set on a hill and considered to be one of the most beautiful in the entire Coteaux du Tricastin. To reach it, leave Clansayes heading south on the winding D571, then turn right on the D133. After about three kilometres, turn left on the D113, right on the D158, then almost immediately right on the D572. Park near the village walls and walk through the streets and across the square to enjoy the carefully restored buildings and quiet, picturesque corners. The village church of St-Michel is Romanesque; its main altar is said to be made from a *taurobole*, a stone block on which bulls were sacrificed during Roman times. There is a magnificent view of the area from the church, but make sure that you also go down to visit the local herb garden, laid out on a terrace on the side of the hill.

Leave La Garde-Adhémar heading eastwards on the winding D572A, a road that leads first through a wooded area. On the way, you could pay a visit to the Chapelle du Val-des-Nymphes, the remains of a plain, 12th-century Romanesque chapel. You will then come to the D133; first turn right, then left towards Chantemerle-lès-Grignan. The remains of a prehistoric dolmen stand in this small winegrowing community, and there is another fine view from the south side of the village near the church. Continue driving east on the D471 to Chamaret. Here, again on the village's south side, stands a 30-metre-high tower on a hill beside some castle ruins. This, too, has been designated as yet another *Tour des Templiers*.

Chamaret marks the end of our route through the Coteaux du Tricastin. Just to the east, by the villages of Grillon and Valréas, is where the Côtes du Rhône wine district begins.

Below *Like many villages in the region, Clansayes is dominated by a* Tour des Templiers, *a legacy from the days of the Knights Templar.*

RECOMMENDED PRODUCERS

BOUCHET
Domaine du Petit Barbaras
A top-class domaine that was
established in 1976.

CAIRANNE
Château le Plaisir
This estate is ranked among the
leading producers at Cairanne.
Cave des Coteaux de Cairanne
Try the Signature series of wines
made at this co-op.
Domaine d'Aéria
The estate makes wines full of
fruit and vanilla tones which taste
better with age.
Domaine Daniel & Denis Alary
These Alarys make good, interesting
white wines in addition to their very
impressive reds.
Domaine de l'Ameillaud
This estate belongs to the Englishman
Nick Thompson.
Domaine Brusset
Daniel and Laurent Brusset make
several good wines. Their Cuvée des
Templiers is especially worth trying.
Domaine Castel Mireio
The firm is run by the
Berthet-Rayne family.
Domaine Catherine le Goeuil
The 1992 vintage was marked by an
intense, fruity nose and a palate full of
complexity, with an elegant structure.
Domaine Delubac
An estate capable of producing
concentrated, beautifully evolved wines.
Domaine du Grand Chêne
One of the leading growers
at Cairanne.
Domaine Marcel Richaud
Interesting Côtes du Rhône and
vins de pays are made by this
independently minded winemaker
who eschews new oak.
Domaine de l'Oratoire St-Martin
Bernard Alary and his sons make
approximately 80% red and 20%
white Côtes du Rhône and Côtes du
Rhône-Villages from their vineyards in
Cairanne. Try the Cuvée Prestige, a
blend of Grenache and Mourvèdre
from very old vines.

THE COTES DU RHONE APPELLATION

Between the Coteaux du Tricastin and an imaginary line
drawn from Orange to Carpentras stretches a vast area
containing thousands of hectares of vineyards. This is the
cradle of the Côtes du Rhône *appellation contrôlée* and of its
superior designation, Côtes du Rhône-Villages.

Stricter standards apply to the latter AC with regard to
grapes planted, yield per hectare and minimum alcoholic
content. In general, therefore, a 'Villages' wine has more
class and concentration than wine that has been classified as
ordinary Côtes du Rhône. The route set out for this area
passes through over 20 villages, most of them belonging to
the Côtes du Rhône-Villages AC.

VILLAGES OF THE COTES DU RHONE

Having stopped at the village of Chamaret on the tour of
the Coteaux du Tricastin, head east on the D471, then the
D64 until you come to a T-junction. Turn right onto the
D941 and head into Grillon, the first stop on our tour of
the villages of the Côtes du Rhône.

Grillon and three of the other *communes* lie within the
so-called *Enclave des Papes*, an isolated part of the Vaucluse
département that is completely surrounded by the *département*
of the Drôme. This strange state of affairs came about when
the Vaucluse Plateau was acquired by the papacy during the
Middle Ages. When the popes were based in Avignon, they
retained ownership of this land (then known as the *Comtat
Venaissin*) and later bought more around the village of
Valréas. The popes wanted to purchase the land in between
their new acquisition and the *Comtat*, but the French king
put a stop to any further purchases by the church, thus
creating an 'island' of papal land – which is why this part of
the Vaucluse is physically located within the Drôme.

The oldest part of Grillon is called *Vialle*, and it is
entered through one of the old town gates that was restored
during the 18th century. The village as a whole was
given fortifications in the Middle Ages, and remains of
these defences include a lookout tower (the clock was

*Right Vines growing near the
town of Valréas. Both the town and
its surrounding landscape belong to
the Enclave des Papes, a part of
the Vaucluse that is actually encircled
by the Drôme département.*

mounted in the 1700s). During the 19th century, Grillon was largely deserted, but – as you can see from your visit – it is inhabited today.

Leave Grillon heading east on the D941 and drive on for about five kilometres until you come to the village of Valréas. With around 9,000 inhabitants, Valréas is the chief village of the Vaucluse *département*. It stands on a hill, its centre surrounded by a ring road lined with plane trees. The streets in the centre of Valréas are narrow, so it is best to go sightseeing by foot. Among its attractions are several houses dating from the Renaissance period, such as the 16th-century Hôtel d'Inguimbert on the northwest side of the Rue Grande. The most beautiful building in Valréas, however, is undoubtedly the elegant Château de Simiane, which was built in the 18th century on the foundations of an old castle. Situated on a pleasant square, it serves today as the town hall and hosts art exhibitions during the summer months. From the château, it is a only few minutes' walk to Place Pie, where the church of Notre-Dame de Nazareth stands; its foundations are medieval but it was built in a mixture of architectural styles and houses a renowned 16th-century organ. West of the church is the older Chapelle des Pénitents Blancs, whose interior has been beautifully decorated with 18th-century woodcarving.

The garden beside the chapel commands a fine view of the old town. To the south of the centre, the 13th-century *Tour de Tivoli* (Tivoli Tower) is all that remains of an earlier fortification, but it serves as a reminder of the power Valréas possessed in feudal times. The past comes to life in other ways within the local *Musée d'Archéologie* (where there is also an aquarium).

One of the most important dates in the history of Valréas was 1317, the year Pope John XXII purchased the town and its vineyards. According to tradition, the acquisition came about because the pope felt his health noticeably improved whenever he drank the local wine. Ever since, on June 23, Valréas has held a festival in the pope's honour called the *Nuit du Petit St-Jean*. As part of the celebrations, a young boy is crowned as the town's patron for a year, and hundreds of people walk through the streets in costume, accompanied by wind bands.

Wine, however, is not the only source of income in Valréas – nor is it even the greatest. Cardboard manufacture, especially of boxes, was developed here in the 19th century, when a local citizen named Ferdinand Revoul began making cardboard boxes for a silkworm breeder. Realising the potential of his new packaging, Revoul created boxes for other businesses; eventually a small box-making factory was established at Valréas. The industry continues to play an important role in the economy of Valréas – which is why the town has an unusual *Musée du Cartonnage et Imprimerie* (Museum of Packaging and Imprinting), situated just outside of town on the road to Orange.

Though small in general terms, the town of Nyons (above) is easily recognized by the Tour Randonne which dominates its skyline.

Domaine Rabasse Charavin
One of the best producers in this part of the Rhône – with one of the few female winemakers, too. Corinne Couturier makes red and white Côtes du Rhône, and Côtes du Rhône-Villages wines from Rasteau, Violes and Cairanne. The Cuvée d'Estevenas is particularly good.

NYONS
Caves Coopérative du Nyonsais
One of the better Côtes du Rhône co-ops, making a range of red, white and rosé wines.

RASTEAU
Cave des Vignerons de Rasteau
The co-op makes good, powerful wines which need age to allow them to reach their full potential.
Domaine MF Bressy-Masson
The only producer of Rasteau *Rancio*: a complex, dry, amber-coloured wine that has been matured for much longer than regular Rasteau and takes on a curious but appealing 'old' flavour as a result.
Domaine des Coteaux de Travers
This estate is run by Robert Charavin, a leading grower in Rasteau.
Domaine de la Girardière
The estate first began bottling its own wines in 1979. Since then, it has gone from strength to strength.
Domaine des Girasols
Extremely well-made wines are produced here, marked by good fruit and spice.

Domaine des Parpaïouns
Didier Charavin produces wines which are elegant and light.

Domaine la Soumade
Here, the highly individualistic André Romero makes Côtes du Rhône, Côtes du Rhône-Villages and a selection of vins doux naturels.

ROCHEGUDE

Cave Coopérative Vinicole de Rochegude
The co-op makes one of the better Villages wines.

Domaine du Gourget
The Tourtin family runs this estate.

SABLET

Cave Coopérative Le Gravillas
Founded in 1935, the co-op makes reliable reds.

Domaine de Boissan
Vacqueyras and Gigondas are made here in addition to Côtes du Rhône.

Domaine Chamfort
Denis Chamfort creates hearty wines with good length at this estate.

Château du Trignon
This estate makes a range of excellent wines.

Domaine Verquière
Produces Côtes du Rhône wines, as well as Vacqueyras.

ST-MAURICE-SUR-EYGUES

Cave des Coteaux de St-Maurice-sur-Eygues
Produces supple, harmonious wines.

STE-CECILE-LES-VIGNES

Cave des Vignerons Réunis
Sells red, white and rosé wines.

Cave Coopérative Vinicole Cécila
Another principal co-op for good Côtes du Rhône wines.

Domaine de la Grand' Ribe
The Sahuc family runs this estate, which is located in the Vaucluse.

Domaine de la Présidente
Max Aubert presides at the Université du Vin in Suze-la-Rousse besides making well-made wines here.

SEGURET

Domaine de l'Amandine
Stop here to try full, fruity wines with a good deal of finesse.

Domaine de Cabasse
There is also a hotel-restaurant at this estate. Try the Cuvée Garnacho.

Les Vignerons de Roaix-Séguret
Round, supple wines may be found at this co-op.

Right *With its covered streets and attractive squares, Nyons – or 'little Nice' as it is sometimes called – is ideal for exploring on foot.*

Leave Valréas by heading east on the D941 (which later becomes the D541) towards Nyons. After about three or four kilometres, you will come to the village of St-Pantaléon-les-Vignes; turn left just after the wine cooperative. Vases, lamps, mosaics and other local artefacts leave no doubt that the Romans once had a settlement here; otherwise, St-Pantaléon-les-Vignes is fairly insignificant – unless, of course, you wish to try some of the wines at the local co-op. As mentioned previously, in many of the villages of the Côtes du Rhône, it is customary for the *cave coopérative* to make practically all the local wine. This is certainly the case at Rousset-les-Vignes, the next destination.

Leave St-Pantaléon-les-Vignes via the country lane that heads northeast towards Rousset-les-Vignes. This makes a pleasant drive – mainly because of the splendid scenery towards the east, which consists of patchwork vineyards and fields set against a dramatic backdrop of brown, rugged mountains.

Rousset-les-Vignes, too, was probably founded by the Romans, and as its name suggests, it has had a long association with wine. Five centuries ago, a register was drawn up dividing the local winegrowing land into three quality categories. The village is scattered across the top and sides of a hill, below what is left of a castle dating from the

14th and 16th centuries; it, in turn was constructed over the remains of an even older fortress. The oldest part of the village is at the top of the hill, hiding in the castle's shadow for protection. Even the church in Rousset has battlements on its towers – sober evidence of the violence of the region's past. The church's interior, however, is more peaceful, and features a fine, 15th-century tombstone of the Abbot Charles for visitors to view, as well as a wooden Renaissance statue of the Virgin.

Leave Rousset-les-Vignes by heading southeast on the D538, and continue on this road to Nyons, the easternmost destination on your journey. Nyons is a relatively small, attractive town nestling in the sheltered valley of the River Eygues, but it seems a huge metropolis in comparison to the wine villages on this route. Its location means that the *mistral* seldom rages here, but around five o'clock on most afternoons, a soft breeze called the *pontias* blows gently through the streets. It brings in some cooler air on hot summer days, and dies down around 10 o'clock in the morning.

In addition to the *pontias*, a unique microclimate makes Nyons warmer than the surrounding countryside – hence the presence of tropical trees and other vegetation around the town. For this reason, the place is sometimes known as *le petit Nice* ('little Nice'). Another nickname is 'the olive capital', for huge amounts of olives (especially the black variety) are harvested in the area, and the industry fuels the local economy. The most important producer of olives and olive oil is the local cooperative, the *Coopérative Agricole du Nyonsais,* on the Place Oliver-de-Serres, which also makes wine. Near the co-op on the Rue des Tilleuls, the *Musée de l'Olivier*, or 'Olive Museum', focuses on the history of the olive tree and the people who cultivate it. There are olive mills at various locations throughout Nyons, and a festival of olives and olive oil is celebrated at certain times during the year.

SUZE-LA-ROUSSE

Château la Borie
La Borie was once owned by the Princes of Orange.

Château de l'Estagnol
Produces well-balanced reds.

Coopérative Vinicole La Suzienne
The co-op makes Coteaux du Tricastin wines in addition to Côtes du Rhône.

TULETTE

Le Cellier des Dauphins
The biggest bottling and marketing concern in the Rhône Valley.

Domaine de la Bérardière
One of Tulette's leading private estates.

Domaine A Mazurd & Fils
Reds from this estate show good fruit and a long finish.

UCHAUX

Château d'Hugues
Makes beautifully balanced, powerful wines.

Château St-Estève d'Uchaux
This château produces delicious wines, including a rosé and a Viognier.

VALREAS

Cellier de l'Enclave des Papes
A large concern that bottles wine from 7 co-ops and numerous estates.

Cave Coopérative La Gaillarde
Founded in 1928, this co-op makes both Côtes du Rhône and Côtes du Rhône-Villages of reasonable quality.

Domaine des Grands Devers
The Sinard family makes sound wines.

Below *The 15th-century Pont Romain, which spans the River Eygues, is thought to be one of the finest arched bridges in Provence.*

Right *Vineyards grow as far as the eye can see in Vinsobres, one of the oldest Côtes du Rhône wine villages.*

Domaine du Val des Rois
Romain Bouchard makes a brilliantly coloured Côtes du Rhônes with a well-balanced palate full of red fruits.

VINSOBRES
La Cave du Prieuré
The younger of the two Vinsobres co-ops, founded in 1959, which ages and sells Côtes du Rhône-Villages wine from Vinsobres.
Domaine de la Bicarelle
One of Vinsobres' leading growers.
Domaine du Coriançon
The red wine is of most interest here.
Domaine de Deurre
Wines from this estate are marked by a palate with a good tannic structure.
Domaine Jaume
A forward-thinking estate with an impeccable cellar.
Domaine du Moulin
Denis Vinson makes lively, beautifully balanced Côtes du Rhône.
La Vinsobraise Coopérative
The older of the two co-ops (founded 1949) concerns itself mostly with red Côtes du Rhône.

VISAN
Cave Coopérative Les Coteaux de Visan
Established in 1937, the co-op still vinifies a good deal of Visan wines.
Domaine de Cantharide
The best *cuvées* rank higher than the usual Villages wines.

WINE FAIRS AND FESTIVALS

● First Sunday in August: wine festival in Valréas.
● Two weeks before Easter: wine festival at Vinsobres.
● Fourth Sunday of July: wine festival at Cairanne.
● Mid-August: Rasteau organises a *Nuit du Vin.*
● Second Saturday in July: wine festival in Visan.
● Third Sunday in August: annual wine festival in Séguret.

HOTELS

La Bellerive
Rasteau
Tel: 4 90 46 10 20
A functional, modern hotel, surrounded by vineyards and close to the wine co-op. It has 20 rooms, a swimming pool and a restaurant.

The best way to explore Nyons is on foot. You can usually park without problems on the Place de la Libération, where all the main roads converge. The *office de tourisme* is situated on this attractive square, as are a myriad cafés and brasseries, fountains and plane trees; games of *boules* are played here in fine weather. East of the Place de la Libération, it is no more than a few dozen steps to the Place du Dr-Bourdongle, an arcaded market square.

Walk straight on from the square, and you will come to the church of St-Vincent, a medieval structure that was restored and enlarged in the 17th and 18th centuries and which currently houses a number of fine paintings. Turn left now and head north through a warren of ancient buildings, covered streets and stairways that characterise the medieval *Quartier des Forts*, or 'Fort Quarter' – the oldest part of Nyons, so-called because of the now-ruined Château Delpinal, a 14th-century feudal castle. The beautiful Rue des Grands Forts is largely covered, and leads to a gateway that was once part of the château. The extraordinary *Tour Randonne* is located in this part of town; the lower part dates from the 13th century and once served as a prison, but the 19th-century priest who became its owner turned it into a chapel. In addition, a curious, neo-Gothic pyramid was constructed on top of the *Tour*, which in turn supports a huge figure of the Virgin Mary. There is also an archaeological museum in the Quartier des Forts.

Walk southwest now to the river, which is spanned by an arched bridge known as the Pont Roman, or 'Roman Bridge', even though it dates from 1409. This bridge – some say it is the finest in Provence – took 70 years to build, and its single arch is 43 metres wide. Nearby, Nyons' love affair with the olive is much in evidence: small shops and showroom windows display olive oil, antique olive presses… even video presentations. Further along the same riverside quay, past a more modern bridge, lies the city's botanical garden, where nearly 200 kinds of aromatic and medicinal plants are grown. Walk back into the town from the garden, keeping straight ahead as far as possible, and you will come back to the *Coopérative Agricole du Nyonsais*, where you can conclude your visit by tasting olives, olive oils – and wines, of course.

To continue the journey, leave Nyons by taking the D94 southwest in the direction of Orange. After about 16 to 18 kilometres, turn right onto the D190 to the village of Vinsobres (the road leads past the Cave du Prieuré, a cooperative cellar where wine is matured). Ahead, to the left, the name of the village is spelled out in large, Hollywood-style letters on a vineyard-covered slope. In 1633, this village name inspired Jean-Marie de Suarès, bishop of Vaison-la-Romaine, to a play on words that urged a moderate consumption of local wine: *Vin sobre ou sobre vin, prenez le sobrement* ('Sober wine or wine of sobriety – take it soberly').

The actual village is quite small, with fewer than 1,000 inhabitants, and – like many in the vicinity – it is set on a hill. Even so, Vinsobres is pleasant to walk through, for its atmosphere is very Provençal. Houses with pastel-coloured shutters cluster around the late 17th-century church, and it is just a dozen paces from here to the cellar of the Jaume wine estate. An even older part of the village lies a bit further up the hill and is entered via a gateway decorated with a sundial. The church here is popularly known as 'the temple'. Four walks have been marked out around Vinsobres; there is a map of them in the centre of the village at the *office de tourisme*, which also serves as a tobacconist's shop.

Leave Vinsobres by heading back on the D94 and continue to travel southwest for about seven kilometres. Along the way you will pass St-Maurice-sur-Eygues, another wine village which occupies a low hillside. Visually, St-Maurice has little to offer, but the local cooperative, which makes most of the local wine, is situated on the west side of the village, should you feel up to wine-tasting.

Continue on the D94 past St-Maurice for three kilometres and turn right onto the D20 to reach the charming old village of Visan. This village used to be encircled by a wall, parts of which still stand – a reminder of the early medieval village that was largely owned (and protected) by one family. As you drive into the centre of

La Caravelle
Nyons
Tel: 4 75 26 07 44
A small (11 rooms), quiet and comfortable place to stay, 10 minutes' walk from the town centre. La Caravelle offers a nice view and a large garden with a terrace where breakfast is served in fine weather. No restaurant.

Château de Rochegude
Rochegude
Tel: 4 75 04 81 88
The Rochegude is a splendid hotel complex that boasts an imposing gateway and courtyard. There are nearly 30 rooms, furnished with antiques and modern comfort. A park, swimming pool and tennis court allow guests to keep fit and work off the inventive cuisine that is served in the château's restaurant. It also commands a pleasant view out over the surrounding countryside.

Colombet
Nyons
Tel: 4 75 26 03 66
The Colombet is located in the heart of town, by the busy Place de la Libération. Most of the nearly 30 comfortable rooms are now soundproofed and air-conditioned. Very tasty, regional dishes – truffle omelettes, lamb, etc – are served in the restaurant. There is also a garage.

Domaine de Cabasse
Séguret
Tel: 4 90 46 91 12
The Cabasse enjoys a quiet location among vineyards, with a nice view of the village. There are 10 pleasant rooms and a restaurant which offers country cooking and wines from its own estate.

Le Grand Hôtel
Valréas
Tel: 4 90 35 00 26
Situated by an intersection on the ring road, this hotel offers 15 fairly large, country-style rooms which have been modernised and double-glazed. You can feast on traditional cuisine in the restaurant.

Hostellerie du Vieux Château
Sérignan-en-Comtat
Tel: 4 90 70 05 58
Separated from the main road by a small park, the Hostellerie boasts 7 pleasant rooms. There is also a rustic dining room where such country dishes as *poulet de ferme farci, aux morilles et à la crème* are served.

Hôtel du Comte
Suze-la-Rousse
Tel: 4 75 04 85 38
A stylishly furnished, country hotel with 11 modern rooms. The restaurant is for guests only.

Right *Viticulture is an important
industry throughout the Southeastern
Rhône, but many growers sell their
fruit to local* coopératives, *rather
than vinify it themselves.*

La Picholine
Nyons
Tel: 4 75 26 06 21
Situated on a hill, and surrounded
by a park with ancient olive trees,
this quiet hotel has about 15 good,
modern rooms, as well as a
swimming pool and a restaurant.
Le Relais
Ste-Cécile-les-Vignes
Tel: 4 90 30 84 39
The Relais is perfectly maintained and
furnished, and much larger than it
appears, for its 12 rooms lie behind
the restaurant. They are all tastefully
decorated and very comfortable –
and they are air-conditioned. There is
also a fairly small swimming pool, and
a spacious restaurant that looks out
on the garden where you can try
some very good cooking based on
ingredients fresh from the market.
Le Relais du Château
Suze-la-Rousse
Tel: 4 75 04 87 07
This is a reliable place, set in a large
park amid vineyards. Guests can
choose from nearly 40 simple but
comfortable rooms, and there is a
swimming pool in addition to the
tennis courts. The air-conditioned
restaurant offers grilled dishes, salads
and country fare.

RESTAURANTS
Au Charbonelon
Rousset-les-Vignes
Tel: 4 75 27 91 61
Stop here for reliable, regional cuisine.
Auberge des Papes
Grillon
Tel: 4 90 37 43 67
Provençal and truffle specialities
are the order of the day here; also
fondue. The restaurant itself boasts
an old-fashioned interior, but its
few hotel rooms were renovated
in 1994. Swimming pool. Near a
junction on the D941.
L'Auberges du Petit Bistrot
Vinsobres
Tel: 4 75 27 61 90
This bistrot is located by the church
square, where it serves affordable,
regional dishes.

Visan, you will pass through the *Porte Puybaret*, or 'Puybaret
Gate', which dates from 1320. In the Middle Ages, the
village was noted for its château, but it was destroyed during
the 16th century, and today all that is left are castle ruins. A
quiet square in the upper (and oldest) part of the village
surrounds the 17th-century church, and the square, in turn,
is surrounded by a series of narrow, circular streets and
several rather crooked old houses, some with rickety-
looking overhead passageways.

The Cave Coopérative Les Coteaux de Visan is situated at
the bottom end of the village and has an excellent reputation.
During the co-op's construction in 1937, many Roman
objects were discovered, including jars and pots that the local
vignerons are certain were used for winemaking. They are
probably right, for winemaking has a long history in Visan;
contemporary archives mention a local wine press in 1250, and
it was around the same period that the church of Notre-Dame
des Vignes – 'Our Lady of the Vines' – was built beside the
D20, in what was then a small grove of trees surrounded by
vineyards. Every year on September 8, the villagers of Visan
make a pilgrimage to this church to attend special masses; there
is also a general blessing of the vines. Notre-Dame des Vignes
has a richly decorated interior, and on the chancel arch are
carved the Latin words *Posuerunt me custodem in vinae* – 'They
have appointed me guardian of the vines'. The figure of the
Virgin in the chapel dates from the 13th century, but the
sublime gilded woodcarving is 500 years younger.

Leave Visan by heading southwest on the D576, then
turn right back on the D94, which leads to Tulette, the
village where Le Cellier des Dauphins, the largest wine firm
in the whole Rhône Valley, is established. This concern
buys and bottles wines from around ten *caves coopératives* in
the local area. Tulette once had walls around it, and the
village church stands by the remnants of one of them, with
a ruined castle close by. Tulette also boasts the *Musée de la
Figurine*, for those who may have a penchant for statuettes.

From Tulette, a narrow road, the D251, runs northwest
through vineyards to the neighbouring village of Bouchet.
Le Cellier des Dauphins makes itself felt here, too, for the

firm bought the remains of a Benedictine abbey; today, hundreds of casks of wine stand in what used to be the refectory and the dormitory. This religious house was originally founded for nuns in the 12th century by a princess of Orange. Two hundred years later, it was plundered and subsequently abandoned, but eventually it passed into the ownership of the abbey of Aiguebelle, which partly restored it; later, a silk factory was set up there. Visitors may tour the imposing, vaulted halls free of charge and taste some of the Cellier's wines. Bouchet's other attractions include the 17th-century chapel of St-Sébastien and, under the *mairie* (town hall), an old *lavoir*, or public washhouse.

Leave Bouchet via the D251 and drive west to Suze-la-Rousse. In 1977, a *Université du Vin* (University of Wine) was established in the local castle, which rises high above the roofs here, dominating the village skyline.

A former hunting seat of the princes of Orange, the castle's oldest section consists of an austere medieval keep, but more attractive-looking wings were added in later centuries, including the Renaissance – which means that this former military bastion was given a splendid Italianate inner courtyard complete with arcades, balustrades and fine sculpture. (Note, too, its fantastic acoustics.) Visitors to the castle can also admire its large staircase, kitchen, dining hall, and armoury, as well as an octagonal drawing room; part of the Université du Vin can be seen on request. Surrounding the castle is a 20-hectare park with a 15th-century 'fives' court, where a game similar to squash or handball was played. In addition, you are free to stroll through the *Jardin des Vignes* (Garden of Vines), which has been planted with around 80 different grape varieties.

As if the castle were not enough, Suze-la-Rousse itself is a charming village full of quaint, narrow streets. Among its sights are the *Halle aux Grains* (Grain Market), the chapel of St-Torquat, the former *hôtel de ville* (town hall) and, again, an old washhouse. Legend has it that the name *Suze-la-*

Le Beaugravière
Mondragon
Tel: 4 90 40 82 54
Mondragon is a typical main-road village on the N7, 15 minutes' drive from Rochegudè. Beside a slight bend in this road, chef Guy Jullien and his wife, Tina, run a good, fairly small, austere-looking restaurant. Regional fare is the speciality – such as, in season, *marmite de cèpes* and creations with truffles. The wine list is amazing, with a magnificent collection of bottles from the whole of the Rhône Valley (there are more than 10 pages of it, with Châteauneuf-du-Pape, many different Hermitages and various vintages of Château Grillet to mention just a very few). There are also a few simple hotel rooms – fortunately, located at the back.

Castel Mireio
Cairanne
Tel: 4 90 30 82 20
This village inn offers good cooking and many local wines.

La Croisée des Chemins
Vinsobres
Tel: 4 75 27 61 19
The cooking is adventurous here, and it's of a good standard to boot. Friendly service and a terrace add to the charms of this restaurant, which is situated just outside the village near the Cave du Prieuré.

L'Etrier
Valréas
Tel: 4 90 35 05 94
This small establishment features a talented chef, whose creations are always based on fresh ingredients.

Below The village of Tulette is home to Le Cellier des Dauphins, the largest wine firm in the Rhône, which bottles wine from ten local co-ops.

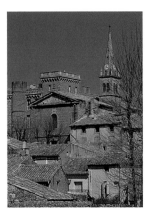

Once famous for its white wine, the village of Rochegude (above) today produces mainly red Côtes du Rhône-Villages.

Rousse is derived from the Celtic *uz*, meaning 'rise' or 'height'; the second element, *La Rousse* – 'the red-haired one' – was the nickname of a local beauty and was probably added later.

Head south now for about five kilometres on the D117 to the village of Rochegude. This village is surrounded by dense vineyards, so it is not surprising to find that a statue of Bacchus was found here, indicating that the Romans made wine in the locality. Today, Rochegude produces mainly red Côtes du Rhône-Villages (most of the vines are Grenache), but in the late-18th and early 19th centuries, white wine was the speciality. While visiting France, future American president Thomas Jefferson (1743-1826) compared white Rochegude to the best white wine from Lisbon; it is said that he was so impressed with it that he sent a few bottles to George Washington. The vines for that wine were brought here from Spain by the Marquis Robert d'Aquéria, who owned the village. His elegant château is still intact, and functions now as a luxurious hotel-restaurant.

From Rochegude, continue heading southwest on the D117, which leads through vineyards and thick woodland to the Commune d'Uchaux, a hamlet that is characterised by its restored dwellings made of soft, Provençal stone.

From Uchaux, you can continue the journey either to Orange (*see* page 111), or turn east onto the D172 and head for the village of Sérignan-du-Comtat. The route to Sérignan leads past an important Côtes du Rhône estate, Château St-Estève d'Uchaux, where visitors are given a warm welcome.

The village of Sérignan itself deserves a visit, for it contains an interesting medieval centre complete with gates across some of its narrow streets. There is also a small museum devoted to the sculptor and painter, Werner Richter-Aix (1939-1987), and a house once occupied by Diane de Poitiers, who became baroness of Sérignan. For naturalists, however, it is the south of the village (on the outskirts, facing towards Orange) that holds the most interest, for this is where renowned entomologist Jean-Henri Fabre (1823-1915) lived and worked. Known as 'the Homer of the insects', Fabre wrote ten books of elegant observations about their complex lives. Although shunned by many of his contemporaries because of some disagreements with Darwin, Fabre has been at least partly vindicated in modern scientific circles, and the citizens of Sérignan are justly proud of him. His body lies buried in the local graveyard, his statue stands in the village square, and his house (on the D976 at the edge of the village) serves as a museum, where visitors can see his laboratory and primitive research equipment, and enjoy his wild, unspoiled garden.

From Sérignan, head northward on the D976. On the way, you will pass through a broad, winegrowing plateau, with the Dentelles de Montmirail and Mont Ventoux outlined in the distance, before reaching the village of Ste-Cécile-lès-Vignes.

La Ferme du Champ-Rond
Valréas
Tel: 4 90 37 31 68
La Ferme is a charming old farmstead where you can enjoy modern interpretations of classic dishes.

Le Mesclun
Séguret
Tel: 4 90 46 93 43
Le Mesclun is a pleasant little place in the old part of the village, with good cooking. You can often eat out on the terrace.

Le Petit Caveau
Nyons
Tel: 4 75 26 20 21
This is a centrally located restaurant, the best Nyons has to offer. It features marvellous regional dishes in addition to more refined creations, all presented in a vaulted, atmospheric dining room.

La Table du Comtat
Séguret
Tel: 90 46 91 49
An excellent, fairly classic restaurant in 15th-century premises, with a great view from the dining room. It is also a small but luxurious hotel complete with swimming pool.

There were people living on the site of Ste-Cécile-lès-Vignes in prehistoric times, but there is no written record of the place until the 12th century. In fact, it used to be called *Cécile-la-Montagnarde*; the present wine-related name only came into being in 1920. After passing one of its two wine co-ops, the Coopérative Cécilia, you come into the main street, which is shaded by plane trees. A short turning on the right, also lined with plane trees, leads to the church of Ste-Cécile, a medieval structure that did not acquire its present form (including the rose window in the west front) until 600 years after it was founded. To get back into the main street, head straight from the church; on the corner you will find the tasting and sales room, or *caveau*, of the Coopérative Cécilia, where you can try the local wines.

Ste-Cécile boasts many fine houses dating from the 16th, 17th and 18th centuries; some of them have intricately carved doorways. Further along the main street stands the Tour de l'Horloge, which originally formed part of a 14th-century defensive wall that encircled the village. Nearby lies the Quartier du Peyron where excavations are being carried out. In addition to its wine, Ste-Cécile also bottles mineral water from local natural springs.

You can see part of the village of Cairanne from Ste-Cécile, for Cairanne is set on a hilltop, and its raised bell-tower dominates the surrounding countryside as well as the village itself. To get there, leave Ste-Cécile heading southeast along the D8.

Because of its strategic position, Cairanne was fought over time and again, and traces of its fortifications are still visible, including parts of the town walls and a gate. Given its reputation as one of the top villages allowed to use the Côtes du Rhône-Villages designation, it is not surprising to find a wine museum in Cairanne, housed beside the village church in what was once a defensive

LOCAL ATTRACTIONS
- Saturday is market day in Grillon.
- On a Sunday in late May, Grillon celebrates a festival of lambs and asparagus.
- First Saturday and Monday of August (or the last in July): a lavender parade drives through Valréas.
- Markets are held on Wednesdays and Saturdays in Valréas. Between November and February, truffles are sold on Wednesdays.
- First weekend of July: village festival in Rousset-les-Vignes.
- Easter weekend: Flower procession in Nyons.
- The Sunday before July 14: the festival of *Les Olivades* takes place in Nyons.
- Thursday is market day in Nyons, with flowers on sale in season.
- Friday is market day in Visan.
- Monday is market day in Tulette.
- Friday is market day in Suze-la-Rousse.
- Saturday is market day in Ste-Cécile-les-Vignes.

Below Cairanne still occupies a strategic position. In addition to its ancient buildings and fortifications, the village also boasts a wine museum.

Above *The main square in Rasteau, a village that welcomes walkers and wine-lovers alike.*

tower of the Knights Templar. In addition to the wine museum's exhibits, the tower affords a fine view of the surrounding countryside.

The oldest part of Cairanne, set high on the hill, is still lived in. One of its most ancient buildings, with weathered stonework and a clock that strikes the hour, was formerly the house of historian Frédéric Alary (1900-1987). Two chapels were built in Cairanne after outbreaks of the plague: Notre-Dame des Excès (1629), on the western slope, and St-Roch (1721). A third, modern chapel was built in 1962 to commemorate the citizens of Cairanne who died in the Second World War. Its stained-glass windows are particularly noteworthy. This chapel stands beside the local wine cooperative, the Cave des Coteaux de Cairanne, one of the larger co-ops in the whole Côtes du Rhône AC.

Travel a few more kilometres east from Cairanne along the D69, and you will come to Rasteau, a village with a definite Provençal air that welcomes wine-lovers and walkers alike. A three-kilometre *sentier viticole*, or 'wine trail', was established here in 1990, using signposts marked with a vine-leaf to point out different routes, and larger signposts to provide detailed information about the sights on the walk. One needs such details, for not only does Rasteau come within the Côtes du Rhône-Villages appellation, it also produces two kinds of *vin doux naturel*, for which it holds a separate AC.

This is a fortified sweet wine, the fermentation of which is interrupted by adding alcohol. In both types, Grenache is nearly always the basic grape. The skins are not fermented with the grapes to make the orange-brown *doré* type of *vin doux*, but they are for the much less common *rouge*. Either way, the style at its best can resemble a light port and can be quite refreshing in its way. At its worst, however, it can be coarse and rough.

Vin doux naturel accounts for approximately a third of all wine made at Rasteau; the rest is Côtes du Rhône-Villages or simple Côtes du Rhône table wines.

It is common for the local *vignerons* to congregate in Rasteau's main square for a game of *pétanque*; not so long ago, their wives would be gathering at the same time at the local *lavoir*, or communal washhouse, to do the weekly laundry, and a few of the older residents still carry on this custom. Meanwhile, the remains of an 11th-century castle stand like a sentry over the little brown-roofed town. Today, one of its buildings houses a wine-tasting centre, complete with laboratory, which is used for official sampling.

From Rasteau, carry on along the D975 to the attractive medieval village of Roaix. On the way, you will pass a *Musée du Vigneron*, (Museum of the Winegrower) where many old winemaking implements are displayed – a sort of introduction to Roaix' long winemaking history. Pliny mentions the Ouvèze Valley's wines as early as AD77, and it is not too far-fetched to suppose that wine has been made in the area ever since. Due to its smaller size, Roaix has

Brown-roofed houses and narrow streets give Rasteau a Provençal air, which is complemented by its ancient church and tower (below).

linked itself to the larger village of Séguret ever since the Cave Coopérative de Roaix-Séguret was established in the latter village in 1960; both villages received the Côtes du Rhône-Villages AC in 1967.

Once in the village itself, Roaix' most noticeable edifice is a 14th-century castle with pink walls and a round tower. It is more curious than beautiful, and privately owned. The 18th-century village church stands on the same hill, but the smaller chapel of Notre-Dame des Crottes is a legacy of the Knights Templar.

From Roaix, take the D7 across the River Ouvèze and head south for about five kilometres to Séguret.

One of the most photogenic villages in the entire Rhône Valley, Séguret is a small, medieval settlement nestled against an almost sheer, rocky hillside and thus suitable for visiting only on foot. Above it are the remains of a medieval fort. The village's narrow, often cobblestone streets climb up to the tenth-century church of St-Denis. The surrounding cluster of houses, as well as the belfry (which has an intriguing one-handed clock) and fountain, are very old; some date from medieval times.

The view from Séguret, facing west towards Orange, is marvellous, and provides a good overall impression of the vineyards in this part of the Rhône. Like Roaix to the north, Séguret's history is intertwined with winemaking from its earliest days. Wine was especially important to the village in the Middle Ages, as 13th-century records of vineyards owned

Below Séguret huddles against its rocky hillside. The medieval village is one of the most photogenic in the entire Rhône Valley.

by a local nobleman, the Comte de Toulouse, testify. Nowadays, though, most *vignerons* grow fruits and vegetables in addition to wine grapes in order to supplement their living.

Just south of Séguret on the D23 lies the much larger village of Sablet, a fortified town built in terraces up a hillside and radiating around its medieval church. As is usual in this part of the Rhône, the oldest section of the village is the highest part, surrounded by a wall. The best way to get to it is to leave your car on the square, which is surrounded by fairly modern buildings, and then negotiate the winding streets on foot.

Unlike Séguret, wine is a definite economic force in Sablet, where it has played an important role for hundreds of years. The village won its Côtes du Rhône-Villages status in 1974, but wine has been made here on a regular basis since the early 16th century. Three hundred years later, Sablet grabbed the international wine world's attention when one of its residents, François-Frédéric Leydier, invented a device which enabled American rootstocks to be grafted onto French vines, thus thwarting the phylloxera epidemic. Today, the local co-op, as well as several independent domaines, makes good wines from the vines grown in the surrounding sandy soil. You can taste some of them in the square at the Caveau des Vins de Sablet and also at the *bureau de tourisme*.

From Sablet, it is only a short drive back to the main D977, which will take you north to Vaison-la-Romaine, where this part of the journey ends.

Below *In Sablet, wine plays an important part in the economy, and good examples of it can be found in the local* coopérative.

RECOMMENDED PRODUCERS

Domaine du Gros-Pata
A reliable producer of Côtes
du Rhône.
Domaine de St-Claude
Makes supple, well-developed wines.

HOTELS
Le Beffroi
Tel: 4 90 36 04 71
This stylish, 16th-century hotel is
situated in the medieval part of
Vaison, near the market square. Its
20, generous-sized rooms are
furnished with antiques which
complement the building itself. The
hotel also has a garden and a terrace,
as well as a good restaurant with
surprisingly reasonable prices.
Le Burrhus
Tel: 4 90 36 00 11
Le Burrhus is quite a modern hotel
located in the heart of the town,
above some cafés – so don't stay here
if you're looking for peace and quiet.
It has 22 rooms and a restaurant,
where guests are served a set menu.
La Fête en Provence
Tel: 4 90 36 36 43
This remarkable hotel, artistically
decorated and furnished, is located
on the market square in the *haute
ville*. It has 7 pleasant rooms and a
good restaurant which features game
on the menu.

RESTAURANTS
Le Bateleur
Tel: 4 90 36 28 04
The Bateleur is situated in the centre,
in the Place Aubanel, and serves good
regional dishes at moderate prices.
La Fête en Provence
Tel: 4 90 36 36 43
See hotels.

VAISON-LA-ROMAINE

A century ago, the town of Vaison-la-Romaine was not
listed in major guidebooks, for it only came to the world's
attention in 1907, when archaeologists began unearthing
the patrician Roman city of *Vasio* in modern Vaison's
Quartier du Puymin. This is the reason that, today, large
parts of Vaison-la-Romaine form what amounts to a
unique open-air museum, for the excavations are spread
over 15 hectares within the town's boundaries.

The Romans settled here in the first century BC, but by
then, Vaison had already been inhabited for at least 600
years by the Celtic Voconces and other tribes. The majority
of Roman ruins are situated in the lower part of the town
on the north bank of the River Ouvèze (there is parking
nearby) on either side of the Avenue Général-de-Gaulle. To
the east, in the *Fouilles Puymin* (or Puymin excavations)
remains of a villa show how spacious and comfortable the lives
of well-to-do Romans were – especially when compared to
those of the working classes. In addition, ancient Vaison
boasted a public promenade; the *Nymphaeum*, which was the
town's fountain and water source; and a fine theatre set on a
hillside – all evidence of a highly civilised and cultured town
of the Roman upper classes.

A museum has been established within the Quartier de
Puymin, where jewels, coins, weapons, oil lamps, toys and
glass are on display. Here, too, are some exquisite statues of
the emperor Hadrian and his wife, Sabina, Caligula,
Tiberius and others, as well as a head of Venus – and there
is a remarkable silver bust of a patrician citizen who lived in
one of the villas. Copies of statues line the paths outside.
The Quartier de la Villasse, to the west, was undoubtedly
the commercial heart of the Roman town: excavations here
revealed a street of shops, public baths, and an intriguing
public toilet that could accommodate a whole family.
Floors, dressed stones and columns indicate the site of the
house of a Roman aristocrat.

Unfortunately, in 1992, the River Ouvèze burst its
banks, killing 30 people and flooding much of Vaison,
damaging a good deal of the excavation work in the
process. Restoration has since returned the ruins to some of
their former glory.

To the west, down the Chemin Couradou, the former
cathedral of Notre-Dame-de-Nazareth stands in a more
'modern' section of Vaison. Its interior, which includes a
small museum and some medieval cloisters, was also badly
damaged in the floods of '92, but the exterior remains a
good example of Provençal Romanesque architecture.

The Pont Romain, a Roman bridge that defied the
flood and is still in use, forms one of the two connections
with the south bank of the Ouvèze; from here, the Rue du
Pont leads upward into the medieval heart of Vaison, which
developed from the 12th century onwards. Steep, zigzag
streets lead up a considerable hill and past the Gothic gate
to the *haute ville*, which is crowned with the impressive

remains of the castle of the Comtes de Toulouse. In its day, this was the largest fortress in the region, and the view from it is splendid, with Mont Ventoux rising in the distance. Many of the streets in this part of the town are paved with stones from the river valley, and the squares are filled with flowers and fountains. Normally, this area is the more sedate part of Vaison, filled with stately 16th- and 17th-century dwellings, but on Tuesdays, the weekly market adds some life to its quiet streets – a tradition that continues to link modern Vaison with its medieval past.

From Vaison-la-Romaine, re-trace your route along the D975 to Orange, where the final tour in this guide begins in the Southern Rhône.

Below *The normally sedate haute ville of Vaison-la-Romaine, which comes to life on market day.*
Below, left *Roman ruins abound everywhere in Vaison, but such was not always the case. The town did not achieve any recognition until excavations began in 1907.*

The Southern Rhône

Without doubt, Châteauneuf-du-Pape is the most famous of all southern Rhône wine appellations. And why shouldn't it be? History, thanks largely to the popes of medieval Avignon, first put its name on the map, and its wines have kept it there ever since. While the reds have traditionally attracted the most attention, white Châteauneuf is fast gaining ground – and rightly so. Yet, just as there is much more to be seen in this part of the Rhône than the city of Avignon, there is much more to southern Rhône wine than Châteauneuf-du-Pape.

Surrounding the town of Orange, which rivals Avignon in historical significance – albeit from Roman, rather than papal times – good, intriguing and individual wines may be found from such west bank appellations as Tavel and Lirac, where rosé plays a much more dominant role. Joining them are other west bank villages which produce their own versions of Côtes du Rhône and Côtes du Rhône-Villages – wines which reflect the very different, dry and less-hospitable *terroir* of the west bank, and are well worth discovering for their individual characters and good value for money.

Individualism on a grander scale can be tasted in two *appellations contrôlées* to the east of the River Rhône: Gigondas and Vacqueyras. In the former, powerful, deep reds are the name of the game, while wines from the latter AC incorporate a greater degree of finesse. Close to these two heavyweights lies the town of Beaumes-de-Venise, where, in addition to Côtes du Rhône-Villages, luxurious dessert wines are produced from the aromatic Muscat grape. Finally, the southern Rhône offers the decidedly lighter, fresher wines of the ruggedly beautiful Côtes du Ventoux appellation.

Wines from all regions of the Rhône Valley were once borne down the river to the historic city of Avignon. This, too, is where our journey ends.

Small in size, but big in wine, Gigondas (left) has lent its name to one of the great southern Rhône reds.

In Tavel (above), rosé is the speciality, proving that there is much more to this part of the region than Châteauneuf.

109

ORANGE

Ask about the earliest inhabitants of Orange, and the first answer is likely to be 'Roman' – despite the fact that this is technically incorrect. *Arausio* was what the Celts in this part of Provence called the capital city they founded in pre-Christian times, but because they left no written records, few people remember them. When the Romans finally did arrive in Orange in 105BC, they were crushingly defeated by two Germanic tribes. It was three years before the Roman general Gaius Marius could take revenge for this embarrassment at Aix, and thousands of Teutons were slain or taken prisoner as a result. Afterwards, the emperor Augustus annexed Orange as a sort of retirement village for veterans of the Second Legion. It was they who built the former Celtic capital into a thriving Roman metropolis on what was then called the *Via Agrippa*, or Agrippa's Way, the road from Arles to Lyon which has since become the N7.

Orange is still thriving today, and its Roman heritage is still largely in evidence. The city's most important monument from that period is undoubtedly the *Théâtre Antique*, a Roman theatre built in the southern part of town (on the Place des Frères-Mounet). In its heyday, it could hold an audience of 10,000 – making it the largest theatre of its kind in Europe, and probably the best-preserved Roman theatre in the world. It is certainly the only one with its stage wall, or *scena*, still standing; at 103 metres wide by 36 metres high, this red sandstone edifice is so impressive that it moved Louis XIV to call it 'the finest wall in the kingdom'. In the centre of the *scena* is a niche from which a larger-than-life-size statue of the emperor Augustus glowers down centre stage. Such was the expertise of the builders of the Orange theatre that its acoustics allow contemporary performers to mount plays and concerts in summertime – without the use of microphones.

Across the street from the theatre entrance is the *Musée Municipal*, the town museum. All manner of relics from Roman times are displayed here, including a unique property register and land survey of the town from 77BC.

Below *A bird's-eye view of Orange. From the air, the size of the Roman amphitheatre is even more impressive.*

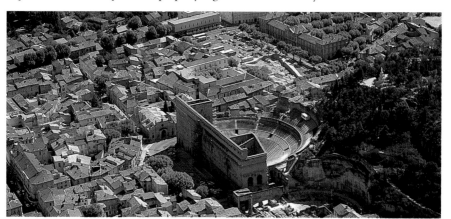

Above *The Arc de Triomphe, Orange-style. Situated in the north of the city, it has managed to survive centuries of wear and tear – including modern pollution.*

ORANGE

HOTELS

Arène
Place de Langes
Tel: 4 90 11 40 40
This stylish, fairly cosy hotel is situated in the city centre and offers 30 rooms. No restaurant.

Le Cigaloun
4 Rue Cariste
Tel: 4 90 34 10 07
The Cigaloun is located near the Roman theatre, and it is a welcoming hotel with around 30 comfortable rooms, but no restaurant.

RESTAURANTS

Le Garden
Place de Langes
Tel: 4 90 34 64 47
Located on the same square as the Arène hotel (see above), the Garden offers delicious, nourishing fare. Truffle soup is often on the menu.

Le Parvis
3 Cours Pourtoules
Tel: 4 90 34 82 00
Situated close to the Roman theatre (and a garage car park), this is the best place to eat in Orange. Inventive dishes are served in stylish surroundings, accompanied by a good wine list with plenty of regional wines.

Just west of the theatre, the remains have been found of a temple and what some archaeologists believe was a large gymnasium; others say it was a forum or circus complex. Whatever it may have been, the ruins extend under a considerable section of the present city centre.

Orange's second major monument is an imposing Roman triumphal arch, situated in the north of the city on a roundabout in the middle of the busy N7. Despite centuries of wear and tear – not to mention modern pollution – it is still in good condition and is the third-largest arch of its type in the world. Above its three openings stand sculptures commemorating Roman victories over the Gauls (the friezes on the north side of the arch are easiest to see).

So much for Roman Orange, but to understand the present city, a bit more history is necessary.

A seat of the counts of Orange (a title created by Charlemagne in the eighth century), Orange passed into Dutch hands 800 years later when it became the property of the Dutch Republic set up by William I, Prince of Orange. In 1622, another prince of Orange, Maurice of Nassau, provided fortified walls for the town and strengthened its castle; unfortunately, he recycled stone from most of the surviving Roman monuments for the purpose, and these have thus disappeared for ever. Orange finally passed into French control after the Treaty of Utrecht in 1713, but – almost as if in tribute to the city it once owned – the Dutch royal family still includes 'Orange' in its name, and the colour has become emblematic. (More information about the history of the princes of Orange can be found on the first floor of the *Musée Municipal*.)

History lessons aside, there is plenty to see and enjoy in contemporary Orange from a simple sightseeing perspective. The city centre is not large and it can easily be explored on foot, starting from the theatre or the museum. (There is an underground car park beneath the Cours Pourtoules; follow the *P Théâtre* signs). Just east of the Roman theatre stands the church of St-Florent, which has a gilded altar that dates from the time of Louis XIV. Alternatively, walk north along the narrow Rue Caristié towards the old town and you will soon come to the former cathedral of Notre-Dame-de-Nazareth. Built at the beginning of the 13th century, it was largely devastated in the religious wars but was restored much later. Most of the works of art inside, including a statue of Christ and the high altar, date from the 17th and 18th centuries. Just west of the cathedral, the Rue Victor-Hugo offers a number of fine buildings before it leads into the Avenue de l'Arc de Triomphe.

For the best overall view of the city, head for the top of the St-Eutrope hill, south of the Roman theatre. You can get there on foot by following a path either from the top of the Cours Aristide-Briand, Montée Place de Chalons, or from the Cours Pouroules, Montée Albert Lambert. Alternatively, you can travel up by car, or in a little train that departs near the theatre (it goes all around the town, with commentary provided). The early inhabitants of Orange had fortifications on St-Eutrope, but the ruins at the top belong to the ill-fated 17th-century castle of the Princes of Orange, which was destroyed by Louis XIV. As if in silent protest to all such wars, a large statue of the Virgin (1857) stands watch on the northernmost point of the hill.

Often known as the gateway to Provence, the city of Orange makes a good base from which to explore the wine villages of the southern Rhône, beginning with its most famous, Châteauneuf-du-Pape.

Below *The huge stage wall of the* Théâtre Antique *so inspired Louis XIV that he declared it to be 'the finest wall in the kingdom'.*

RECOMMENDED PRODUCERS

Domaine Lucien Barrot et Fils
The estate makes powerful wines,
with notes of tobacco and spice.

Domaine de Beaurenard
High quality is the hallmark of Paul
Coulon and his sons, who produce
big, complex, fruity reds.

Domaine du Bois Dauphin
Makes well-structured wines.

Henri Bonneau
One of the top producers of
Châteauneuf-du-Pape.

Le Bosquet des Papes
Maurice Boiron runs this well-
respected, smaller estate.

Les Cailloux
André Brunel has made Les Cailloux
into one of Châteauneuf's top
domaines, with finely structured
whites and full, fruity reds.

Caves St-Pierre
Although this firm is geared to mass
production, it nevertheless supplies
a number of good wines.

Château Cabriéres
The estate produces good white
as well as good red Châteauneuf.

Domaine Chante-Cigale
The name means 'singing grasshopper';
the wine is traditional in style.

Domaine Chante-Perdrix
This one means 'singing partridge'.
Its wines are powerful and fine.

Les Clefs d'Or
Jean Deydier and sons make good,
traditional wines here.

Clos du Mont Olivet
Run by the Sabon brothers, who
make Côtes du Rhône as well as
fine red and white Châteauneuf.

Clos des Papes
The Avril family runs things here,
producing equally fine red and
white Châteauneuf from vines
with an average age of 35 years.

La Cuvée du Vatican
Félicien Diffonty and his sons
produce sound, reliable wine.

Domaine Durieu
Run by Paul Durieu, who also makes
good Côtes du Rhône.

Château des Fines Roches
One of the oldest names in
Châteauneuf; also a hotel-restaurant.

Château Fortia
The home of the late Baron Pierre Le
Roy de Boiseaumarie. Today, Pierre's
grandson Bruno runs the estate, trying
to rebuild and consolidate it after
financial difficulties.

Right *The town which launched
a thousand cellars: Châteauneuf-du-
Pape, home of what is probably the
best-known Rhône wine in the world.*

CHATEAUNEUF-DU-PAPE

Head south from Orange on the D68, a less-travelled and more scenic route that avoids the worst of the industrial development nearest the river. After about ten kilometres, you will come to a large village straddling a hill amid a green sea of vines. This is Châteauneuf-du-Pape, the halfway point between Orange and Avignon, and the home of what is probably the best-known southern Rhône wine in the world.

It was here at Châteauneuf that the *appellation contrôlée* system was born in 1923, when a group of local *vignerons*, led by the Baron Pierre Le Roy de Boiseaumarie of Château Fortia, drew up a charter of six stipulations to regulate and safeguard the quality of their table wines. A few years later, these rules became the basis for the French national laws of *appellation d'origine*. Today, over 70 years later, the laws of *appellation contrôlée* remain largely unchanged since Baron Le Roy's time, and have been used by winegrowers throughout Germany, Italy and Spain as a formula by which to regulate their own wine industries.

In the modern Châteauneuf vineyard, over 3,000 hectares are planted with both red and white grapes, mainly in a northwest/southeast oval that stretches from the A7 *autoroute soleil* in the east to the River Rhône in the west. Besides Châteauneuf itself, the appellation takes in the neighbouring *communes* of Bédarrides, Courthézon, Sorgues and Orange. The most prevalent grape variety is Grenache, which accounts for approximately 60 per cent of vines planted, but because it can be unbalanced on its own, another 12 different varieties (including five white ones) are permitted for use in making red wines – and some

producers *do* use all 13 in their blends. White Châteauneuf may use up to six varieties. While the bulk of production consists of red wine, most estates make a modest amount of white Châteauneuf-du-Pape, and its volume (and reputation) has been increasing considerably since the 1980s.

At its best, red Châteauneuf-du-Pape is a broad, generous, sinewy wine boasting all sorts of dark and fruity elements. The white variant often has the generosity of a white Burgundy, with floral, fruity and spicy nuances. It is hardly possible, however, to give general characteristics, for each of the dozens of estates makes its own style of wine. Estate-bottled Châteauneufs can be recognised by the crossed-keys insignia on the neck of the bottle. The wines derive a part of their power and class from the round, red and cream-coloured stones, or *galets*, that cover many of the vineyards. They were apparently left by ancient Alpine glaciers, and the biggest concentrations are found north and northwest of the village itself, on *domaines* such as Château de Beaucastel or Mont-Redon. During the day, the stones absorb the sun's heat, then radiate it during the cooler nights like little ovens, reflecting it onto the vines. As a consequence of this 'central heating' effect, the grapes achieve maximum ripeness. In addition to the *galets*, the vines benefit from the cleansing winds of the *mistral*, which keep them dry and free from pests and airborne diseases such as mildews.

But what of the village which gave this appellation its name? The popes who resided in Avignon for the greater part of the 14th century had a great influence on the provincial capital and its surroundings. The first of these, Clement V, used to ride into Châteauneuf on his mule to

Above *Throughout the appellation, red Châteauneuf-du-Pape benefits from a sojourn in oak barrels.*

Château de la Gardine
Besides its excellent wines, the château also possesses its own lookout tower.

Domaine du Grande Tinel
Excellent wines may be found here.

Domaine du Haut des Terres Blanches
Owned by Rémy Diffonty, who makes agreeable, elegant wine.

Domaine de Marcoux
Philippe Armenier's entire estate is run on bio-dynamic principles, and he produces some marvellous wines. Try the excellent Cuvée Vielles Vignes.

Domaine de Montpertuis
Run by Paul Jeune, Montpertuis offers two red Châteauneufs (Cuvée Classique and Cuvée Tradition) as well as one white. All are top-quality wines.

Château Mont-Redon
One of the great names for red and white Châteauneuf.

Domaine de Nalys
All 13 grape varieties are grown here and used in the wines.

Château la Nerthe
La Nerthe was the first estate to start bottling its own wine, in 1785, and exemplary quality remains its hallmark. Do try its whites – they equal the reds, and show just what white Châteauneuf is like at its best.

Domaine du Pégau
The Feraud family runs this estate – father and daughter are both winemakers – producing solid whites and well-structured reds.

Père Anselme
A *négociant* with a number of good, consistent wines and an interesting museum of wine implements.

Right *Château la Nerthe was the first estate in Châteauneuf to bottle its own wines. It began in 1785, and has not stopped since.*

Château Rayas
At press time, Château Rayas was still coming to terms with the loss of its owner, the indomitable Jacques Reynaud. The domaine is now run by his sister, Françoise, and his nephew, Emmanuel. It is hard to imagine, however, that the top-quality wines will change very much from their traditional, formidable state.

Domaine des Relagnes
Henri Boiron produces full, fruity Châteauneufs from 12ha of vines, and Côtes du Rhône from an additional 3ha.

Domaine Riché
Produces classic wines of good structure.

Domaine la Roquette
Traditional Châteauneuf, made by the Brunier family.

Domaine St-Benoît
The estate bears the name of Pope Benoît XII of Avignon fame. Its wines are well-balanced, with good structure.

Domaine de la Solitude
Solitude has been bottling since 1815. Its 'Vin de la Solitude' became a concept back in the 19th century. The more recent vintages have shown a much-needed return to quality from the disappointing ones of the '80s.

Château de Vaudieu
An 18th-century château with an established reputation.

Le Vieux Donjon
Lucien and Marie-José Michel make deep, complex Châteauneuf wines here, with a minimum of chemical interference. Both reds and whites are worth seeking out.

Château du Vieux Lazaret
Makes Côtes du Ventoux as well as Châteauneuf-du-Pape.

BEDARRIDES
Bérard Père & Fils
Négociant firm with a wine estate, which produces the outstanding Domaine de Terre Ferme.

Domaine Font de Michelle
Wines are improving here; subsequently, the spicy reds and fine whites are not cheap.

Domaine du Vieux Télégraphe
The estate uses a high percentage of Grenache in its blends to create rich, complex wines such as the 1994 Cuvée Prestige.

inspect a vineyard he had planted there. His successor, John XXII, decided to rebuild a neglected castle that already existed at Châteauneuf in order to have a powerful yet comfortable stronghold as part of a line of defence around Avignon – thus allowing the pope an escape from the pressures of city life into the bargain. When John XXII was chosen as pope in 1316, everyone expected his period of office to be short, for he was old, delicate and weak. As it turned out, he remained in office for nearly 17 years; for 15 of them work continued on the new castle, or *château neuf*. It was completed in 1333, a huge, impressive structure, with four large towers rising high above the village and its surroundings. Ironically, Pope John was able to enjoy it for just one year before his death.

Yet John left more than a new château as his legacy. While the castle was being constructed, he had begun planting grapes and olives on the 25 acres of land that went with the property. Soon, his vineyards had become the best-known in the village – despite the fact that villagers had already been growing vines there for 150 years or more. Hence Châteauneuf wine was drunk at the papal court right from the start of the court's existence – including, of course, the reign of John XXII himself. When, on November 22, 1324, he gave a wedding banquet for his great-niece, not only were sheep, pigs, wild boar, chickens, partridges and fish on the menu, there were also 11 casks of wine from Châteauneuf. Written records from the time claim that there were around 3,300,000 vines growing in and around the village – whether or not this is strictly true, there were certainly adequate numbers from which to provide enough wine to quench lavish papal thirsts.

The popes departed Châteauneuf in 1378. While the castle remained in reasonable shape for several decades thereafter, it eventually fell into disrepair. After being plundered, it stood practically empty until it was set on fire during the religious wars of the 16th century. Even then, one tower and the dungeon remained intact until 1944, when the retreating German army blew up most of what was left. Today, only a few parts of the walls remain, as does the dilapidated tower, but even these ruins still manage to convey a glimpse into what must have been an impressive building. From the ruins, there is a fine view of the village and its surroundings. Beneath the tower, a large underground hall is used for local wine events. One has the feeling that John XXII would have approved.

From the ruins, you will see that the village of Châteauneuf-du-Pape lies at the centre of a whole web of roads which converge on a small square beside a 14th-century fountain. There is no doubting that wine is still very much the order of the day here: on a bench beside the fountain, retired growers exchange the latest items of news, and winegrowers' plaques and signs are to be seen everywhere in the village.

Still, man does not live by corkscrews alone – not even in Châteauneuf-du-Pape. At the foot of the castle stands the Romanesque church of Notre-Dame-de-l'Assomption, and there are a few chapels elsewhere in the village, including the 11th-century St-Théodore, to minister to more spiritual values. But even so, there is no escaping the force of the vine in this village. On the Avenue Bienheureux-Pierre-de-Luxembourg, to the south of town on the way to Avignon, sits the wine firm of Père Anselme which also owns the *Musée des Outils de Vignerons* – the 'Museum of Winegrowers' Tools'. Here you can stop to taste the firm's wines and view a fine collection of winegrowing equipment, including a 4,000-litre medieval cask, a 16th-century press – and, of course, a large number of corkscrews.

From Châteauneuf, head west on the D17, then turn left onto the D976 to cross the River Rhône. Continue heading south on this road, past Roquemaure, for about six kilometres, before turning right onto the D4 and heading into Tavel, where our tour through the villages of the west bank begins.

COURTHEZON

Domaine Autard
Paul Autard also makes Côtes du Rhône.

Château de Beaucastel
Belongs right at the top in this district. The brothers Jean-Pierre and François Perrin produce a tremendous red Châteauneuf-du-Pape from separately vinified grape varieties (all 13); also a few choice whites, among them the very expensive Vieilles Vignes.

Le Cellier des Princes
The only co-op in Châteauneuf.

Domaine du Cristia
A leading producer of Châteauneuf.

Domaine de la Janasse
Christophe Sabon makes good Côtes du Rhône and fine Châteauneuf – both red and white. Try the Cuvée Chaupin.

HOTELS

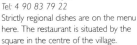

Hostellerie Château des Fines Roches
Tel: 4 90 83 70 23
The Hostellerie comprises a hotel and restaurant, and both are luxurious. Its 6 comfortable rooms are located in a 19th-century château 3km out of the village, surrounded by the vineyards and cellars of the château.

La Sommelerie
Tel: 4 90 83 50 00
Along the route from Roquemaure, this establishment offers 14 very comfortable rooms, a swimming pool and an outstanding restaurant.

RESTAURANTS

La Mule du Pape
Tel: 4 90 83 79 22
Strictly regional dishes are on the menu here. The restaurant is situated by the square in the centre of the village.

Le Pistou
Tel: 4 90 83 71 75
Le Pistou is a good place to stop for regional cooking.

Le Verger des Papes
Tel: 4 90 83 50 40
This agreeable restaurant serves Provençal cuisine and offers a large number of the wines by the glass.

LOCAL ATTRACTIONS
● April 25: Châteauneuf celebrates the Feast of St Mark.
● First weekend in August: the *Fête de la Véraison*, a craft and medieval fair, is held in Châteauneuf-du-Pape.
● Friday is market day in Châteauneuf-du-Pape.

Left *The fairytale towers of Château des Fines Roches conceal a hotel-restaurant as well as one of the oldest wine estates in the area.*

Above *The 'pont' at Pont-St-Esprit. For seven centuries, this was one of just three bridges which crossed the River Rhône.*

THE WEST BANK

The act of crossing over to the Rhône's west bank brings with it an abrupt change in scenery. The rich, green fields of the Vaucluse, broken here and there by cypress trees, have been replaced by an arid landscape of rocky hills. Spread about them are parched rows of vines which struggle to grow in harsh conditions. The dry stretches of countryside are only alleviated by tiny, half-forgotten villages scattered among the valleys and sparse woodland.

Because the wine villages in this area belong to the Gard *département*, they actually come within the Langue-doc region of France. But the Provençal influence is still strong in this part of the country, as is quickly apparent from the architecture and the cooking in the villages concerned. The character of the wines, too, is closer to that of wines from the east bank of the Rhône than to the wines of the Languedoc. Even so, this resemblance does not alter the fact that winegrowers on the west bank have their own specialities, one of the most important of which is undeniably rosé.

Indeed, rosé is the only wine allowed to be produced under the Tavel *appellation contrôlée*, one of the two major west bank ACs. A relatively large amount of rosé is also made in villages such as Chusclan under the Côtes du Rhône and Côtes du Rhône-Villages appellations. The success of rosés in this area can be attributed mainly to climate: the west bank is slightly cooler than the other side of the Rhône. Early *vignerons* were just as aware of this fact as their modern counterparts, with the result that, for centuries, rosé has been a speciality of *communes* like Laudun; the only difference is that today the wines are vinified in a dry style, whereas before, they were made to be primarily sweet.

But more than rosé is produced here, as is easily demonstrated by that other major west bank appellation, Lirac. While good rosé is in fact made in Lirac, fruit-packed reds are also produced, many of which can equal red Châteauneuf-du-Pape. They, along with a lesser amount of white wine, are considered to be the best wines in the entire Gard *département*.

On the whole, the west bank of the Rhône is much less developed in terms of tourism. Most visitors to this part of France elect to stay in the Vaucluse, in the Ardèche or in the Languedoc, using this part of the Rhône Valley mainly as a route to other destinations. On one hand, this is a shame, since, despite its arid appearance, the area does offer some charming villages as well as a number of agreeable hotels and restaurants. However, this lack of popularity is an advantage to the enlightened traveller, for one can more easily get a glimpse into everyday life in the Gard – including 'real' cuisine and good local wines to go with it.

The route described here runs roughly south to north. It begins in the village of Tavel, northwest of Avignon, and ends in Pont-St-Esprit, just southwest of Bollène.

IN AND AROUND TAVEL

'There is no good wine except for Tavel!' Such was the declaration of King Philip the Fair (1268-1314) who, while still on his horse, quenched his thirst with a beaker of the stuff while on a tour of the kingdom. Throughout the centuries, kings, bishops and authors such as Balzac, Brillat-Savarin, Alphonse Daudet and Frédéric Mistral have followed his example and praised Tavel's wines, so it is little wonder that the roof of the local wine cooperative is emblazoned with the words: *Tavel: 1er rosé de France*. Grapes have certainly been made into rosé in this village for hundreds of years – indeed, rosé is the only wine allowed in the Tavel *appellation contrôlée* (which also takes in the neighbouring town of Roquemaure). Yet whether it is still the country's best rosé is open to debate. Styles and quality of the wine vary considerably; often, Tavel can have too hefty a dose of alcohol and not quite enough freshness and fruit – an indication of its (usually) high Grenache content. At its best, however, it can make for a tasty, gluggable, refreshing wine, a good argument against the 'real-wine-lovers-don't-drink-rosé' brigade.

RECOMMENDED PRODUCERS

Château d'Aquéria
Stop here for top-class Tavel rosé and the red and white Lirac, made from vines with an average age of 30 years.
Domaine Corne-Loup
Jacques Lafond produces Lirac in addition to Tavel.
Domaine de la Genestière
Makes outstanding, dry rosé.
Domaine Lafond
You can also find good red Lirac here.
Domaine Maby
Maby Tavel is usually a wonderful expression of *terroir*. The estate also produces a marvellous white Lirac.
Domaine Méjan-Taulier
Makes Lirac alongside its Tavel.

Below *The vines that surround Tavel are most likely to be Grenache and Cinsaut, although at least seven other varieties can be planted.*

Right *While Tavel as a whole is a rather run-of-the-mill village, exploring on foot allows visitors to appreciate its subtle charms.*

Domaine de la Mordorée
First-rate wines may be found here, including Côtes du Rhône.
Prieuré de Montézargues
The origins of this estate go back to the 13th century. Today, it makes exceptional wines.
Domaine de Tourtouil
Michele Lefevre makes good, lively wines at this estate.
Château de Trinquevedel
An attractive château which makes sound wine.
Domaine le Vieux Moulin
Run by the Roudil family.
Les Vignerons de Tavel
The co-op produces about half of all Tavel, plus some Lirac.

DOMAZAN
Château de Domazan
Makes an excellent light red that would be perfect for summer drinking.
Domaine des Romarins
Georges Fabre produces a powerful red Côtes du Rhône that needs age to bring out its best.

SAZE
Domaine de la Charité
The estate is known for its well-balanced rosé.

HOTELS

Auberge de Tavel
Tavel
Tel: 4 66 50 03 41
The Auberge offers around 11 slightly old-fashioned rooms, which are nonetheless stylish and comfortable. There is a swimming pool and a terrace at the back, and a restaurant.

RESTAURANT

Hostellerie du Seigneur
Tavel
Tel: 4 66 50 04 26
A congenial place in the centre of Tavel, which prepares country food with care. Also offers 7 hotel rooms.

The road into the village itself leads past the local cooperative, which vinifies just over half of Tavel's total production. A little further on, dozens of parking places are marked out along the road, so leave the car here and explore the village on foot. Even though it is one of the two most significant *communes* on the west bank of the Rhône (Lirac being the other), Tavel itself is fairly nondescript. It consists of a fairly compact, small centre with narrow, sloping streets, various tasting centres, a public *lavoir,* or washhouse, a jumble of old houses and a grey church with an ancient belfry. Just east of the village, the remains of a Roman settlement have been found, including a pit containing grape seeds, so it is safe to say that vines were cultivated here long ago.

From Tavel, it is about five kilometres south on the D976 to Rochefort-du-Gard, a village that belongs to the standard Côtes du Rhône AC. On the way, you will pass Le Sanctuaire de Notre-Dame-de-Grâce, a group of religious buildings set on a hillside, with cloisters and a small church that usually displays a collection of votive offerings. The village of Rochefort itself is also set on a hillside, with a white, 19th-century church at the very top. The *mairie* (town hall) was once a chapel and has a fine, wrought-iron balcony. Two other pleasant wine villages are situated a little further south of Rochefort. Saze (reached by the D287) is home to such producers as André Payan of Domaine des Moulins, while at Domazan (take the N100 west from Saze then turn south on the D108), you can find the large Château de Domazan estate, which has been making wine since the 14th century.

LIRAC

From Tavel, a narrow road runs north through the surrounding vineyards to Lirac. This small village has lent its name to the other important west bank appellation, which is made up of four *communes*: itself, St-Laurent-des-Arbres, Roquemaure and St-Geniés-de-Comolas. Unlike the Tavel *appellation contrôlée*, which is restricted solely to rosé wines, the Lirac AC covers red, rosé and white wines, all of which can be splendid.

Time was when Lirac used to rival Tavel in terms of rosé, but in the early 1970s, tastes began to change. Today, producers of Lirac look upon red wine as the mainstay of their business. The chief grape varieties for the purpose are Grenache, Syrah, Mourvèdre and Cinsaut, while for whites, Clairette, Bourboulenc and Grenache Blanc are the main varieties. Alcohol levels in both red and white wines are considerably lower than those allowed for Châteauneuf-du-Pape, and the best of them repay keeping for a few years. These are, by all accounts, the best wines the Gard *département* has to offer, with a spicy fruitiness and a firm and supple elegance. Because Lirac is such a little-known appellation, its wines are frequently the best value for money.

All of which makes it seem ironic to find that the village of the same name is a fairly unremarkable place. There are the remains of some defensive walls; a little old church; an austere square with a fountain; and a couple of tasting centres. A road running west from the village leads to a chapel in a cave called the Hermitage de la Ste-Baume. Otherwise, Lirac has the air of a sleepy little village where nothing much happens, and it is hard to believe that good wine has been made here for centuries.

Lirac's surroundings, however, have more to offer. St-Laurent-des-Arbres, for example, which lies north of Lirac on the D26, is noticeably bigger. One of the district's two cooperatives is located here, on the south side of the village. St-Laurent once belonged to the bishops of Avignon, who fortified it in the 14th century; thus, the originally

RECOMMENDED PRODUCERS

Jacques Melac
Situated on the Place de la Mairie.
Château de Ségriés
The château itself is in ruins and the wine is made in cellars built beside it – ironic, really, as it is the only big producer of Lirac located in Lirac itself.

ROQUEMAURE
Château de Bouchassy
A leading grower of Lirac.
**Château St-Roch/
Château Cantegril-Verda**
Both belong to the Verda family. They produce elegant Liracs as well as some Châteauneuf-du-Pape.
Cave Coopérative de Roquemaure
The co-op makes sound Lirac.
Domaine Assémat
Produces various wines, including reds made mostly from Syrah grapes. Names used are Domaine des Causses & St-Eynes, and Domaine des Garrigues.
Domaine des Carabiniers
Christian Leperchois makes a well-structured rosé here.
Domaine Castel-Oualou
Top-class Liracs are the order of the day at this estate.
Domaine de la Croze
Makes white Côtes du Rhône in addition to good Lirac.

ST-LAURENT-DES-ARBRES
Château le Devoy Martine
Stop here for elegant wines.

Below *Unlike Tavel, growers in Lirac can produce red, white and rosé wines – all of which are said to be among the best in the Gard.*

Right *Because the village itself is so quiet and unprepossessing, visitors find it hard to believe that good wine has been produced in Lirac for centuries.*

Cave Coopérative des Vins de Cru Lirac
One of the brands to look out for is Monseigneur de la Rovière.

WINE FAIRS AND FESTIVALS
● August 12 and 13: wine fair in Roquemaure.

HOTELS

Château de Cubières
Roquemaure
Tel: 4 66 82 89 33
Choose from around 20 stylish rooms of varying sizes, complete with silk hangings, flowered wallpaper, antique furniture and other characterful items. There is a restaurant in the same park as the hotel, but under different management (so you pay for your meal there, not at the hotel). It is in a sort of baronial hall with high wooden chairs, and the menu offers both traditional dishes (*l'estouffade de boeuf*) alongside more original ones.

La Galinette
St-Laurent-des-Arbres
Tel: 4 66 50 14 14
This hotel in the old town centre offers 10 rooms with contemporary furnishings. No restaurant.

Hostellerie de Varenne
Sauveterre
Tel: 4 66 82 59 45
A pleasant place to stay in the church square at Sauveterre, a village just south of Roquemaure. It occupies 18th-century premises, but the 14 rooms are provided with modern comforts. There is also an excellent restaurant.

RESTAURANTS

Les Acacias
St-Laurent-des-Arbres
Tel: 4 66 50 32 58
This unpretentious village restaurant and café has an agreeably friendly, relaxed atmosphere.

LOCAL ATTRACTIONS
● Tuesday is market day in Roquemaure.

Romanesque church was also given a more defensive aspect, complementing a 12th-century fortified tower known as the Tour de Ribas which already existed there. The historic little centre of St-Laurent-des-Arbres is also worth a stroll, for the village itself has a very pleasant and genial atmosphere.

Heading east from St-Laurent on the D980 leads to Roquemaure, the largest of the Lirac villages. Near the intersection with the N580 stands a *Maison des Vins* which is basically a sales counter for carefully selected regional wines (and it is open seven days a week).

Situated on the Rhône with nearly 5,000 inhabitants, Roquemaure is the most important *commune* in the district – and indeed, it has a history of importance. Tradition has it that this is the point at which Hannibal crossed the Rhône on his elephant-laden rafts, but in more recent times it was used as a port for more domestic items. In the 18th century, for example, Roquemaure was the largest harbour for shipping wine in the entire Rhône Valley.

You can park without problems near the centre of Roquemaure, in a large square dotted with plane trees. It is then about a minute's walk to the Place de l'Hôtel-de-Ville, where both old and contemporary town halls may be found, as well as a medieval church which contains a marvellous 18th-century organ. Outside the town centre, on an isolated, dark-coloured rock known as the *Roca Maura*, loom the remains of a mighty, eight-towered castle where the first of the Avignon popes, Clement V, died on April 20, 1314.

Because it is mainly a factory town and suffers from the fumes of the local steelworks, St-Geniès, the last of the Lirac villages, is probably best given a detour. From Roquemaure, however, it is only a short drive west to St-Victor-la-Coste, where the next tour begins.

AROUND BAGNOLS-SUR-CEZE

Besides Lirac and Tavel, a number of other wine villages make their homes on the west bank of the Rhône. These belong to the Côtes du Rhône or Côtes du Rhône-Villages *appellations contrôlées* and are situated in the area around Bagnols-sur-Cèze, a city located almost due west of Orange, which itself produces some wine. The village closest to the Lirac appellation is St-Victor-la-Coste, roughly 15 kilometres south of Bagnols, and the starting point for this tour.

To reach St-Victor-la-Coste, follow the D101 west from St-Laurent-des-Arbres. This rather quaint, out-of-the-way hill village lies at the foot of a dismantled castle, from which there is a good view of the countryside. The church in the old part of the village was completed in the 18th century, and was built against a defensive wall. Nowadays, though, there is not much to defend in St-Victor, apart from a quiet way of life. Wine is made at the local co-op, but it shares its Côtes du Rhône-Villages appellation with the larger and more important wine village of Laudun, whose name appears on the wine labels.

Laudun lies about five and a half kilometres north of St-Victor on the D240, and it is one of the four oldest Côtes du Rhône-Villages villages; it has been allowed to use its name on its wines since 1953, the year in which Gigondas, Cairanne and Chusclan were granted the same status. The village seems to stretch up a steep, limestone slope, and the flat area at the top was used for a Roman encampment – it still goes by the name of the *Plateau du Camp de César*. Amphorae from the third and second centuries BC have been found here, and it seems likely that they would have held wine, since vines have always been more commonly cultivated by the locals than olive trees. The tradition continues today, and Laudun produces red, white and rosé wines. While red dominates in terms of volume, Laudun whites are arguably some of the best in the entire southern Rhône – second, according to some experts, only to top whites from Châteauneuf-du-Pape.

RECOMMENDED PRODUCERS

BAGNOLS-SUR-CEZE
Domaine de Lindas
Situated on the road to Pont-St-Esprit, the estate makes reliable Côtes du Rhône.

CHUSCLAN
Cave Coopérative de Chusclan
This excellently equipped estate has plenty to offer. Wines worth discovering include the white Dame de France and the rosé Domaine du Grés Blanc.
Domaine de Cupissol
Try the delicious red Cuvée Gustave Sabot.
Domaine de Signac
The estate is run by the same owners as Château la Nerthe in Châteauneuf-du-Pape.

LAUDUN
Cave des Quatres Chemins
The cooperative has Baronnie de Sabrans as one of its labels.
Château St-Maurice l'Ardoise
Makes reliable Côtes du Rhône.
Cave de Vignerons de Laudun
Produces various qualities of wine. Whites are usually of an exemplary standard, while Domaine Boulas is a decent red wine from a single estate.

ORSAN
Cave Coopérative d'Orsan
The co-op is allowed to make Villages wine using the Chusclan name.

Below *Roquemaure is rich in history. It is said that Hannibal crossed the Rhône here, but in more peaceful times it was an important harbour.*

PONT-ST-ESPRIT
Domaine de Laplagnol
Run by Pierre Coste, and based in
the Quartier Masconil.

SABRAN
Château de Bastet
The château also makes white wine.
Domaine de la Réméjeanne
The Réméjeanne wines show good,
rich fruit as a rule.

ST-ALEXANDRE
Domaine de Roquebrune
Pierre Riqué produces good Côtes
du Rhône here.
Mas Claulian
The Herbouze family arrived from
Morocco in 1962. Today, Claude
Herbouze makes a sound red wine.

ST-GERVAIS
Cave Coopérative de St-Gervais
Produces good red and rosé wines –
and most of the wine in the village.
Domaine Ste-Anne
Located in the hamlet of Les
Cellettes, Ste-Anne makes delicious
wines, among them a red *cuvée* with
a high percentage of Syrah.

ST-VICTOR-LA-COSTE
**Cave Coopérative de
St-Victor-la-Coste**
One of 3 co-ops that make Laudun
Villages wine.
Domaine Estournel
The estate produces white and red
Laudun of high quality.
Domaine Pélaquié
A renowned wine estate, making a
range that includes white Laudun,
and red and rosé Lirac.

VENEJAN
Cave Coopérative de Vénéjan
Red wine is of the most interest here.

WINE FAIRS AND FESTIVALS

• July: Bagnols-sur-Cèze usually holds
a wine fair, at which many growers
set up stalls to offer tastings.

HOTELS

Auberge Lou Caleou
Vénéjan
Tel: 4 66 79 25 16
Fifteen comfortable rooms make up
this establishment, located at the
bottom end of the village.
There is a simple restaurant.
Château de Lascours
Laudun
Tel: 4 66 50 39 61
This well-maintained château
2km from Laudun has 6 rooms.
No restaurant.

A bustling, modern city that is home to many of the
region's factory workers, Laudun nonetheless has its own
historic points of interest. Its massive medieval Gothic
church, for instance, can be seen from miles away. Located
in the old part of town (now ringed by modern houses), it
underwent some renovation around 1825, when the arches
of the nave were replaced and the entire structure had to be
lowered; this explains why its high, narrow windows are
partially filled in. At around the same time that the church
was being renovated, the white wines of Laudun were being
mentioned with praise in various chronicles and guidebooks. No doubt the painter Renoir (1841-1919) sampled
several of them when he stayed at number 81 Rue de
Boulogne on a number of occasions.

On the hill behind the village church stands a chapel
with a statue of the Virgin Mary beside it; this marks the
highest point in Laudun, and it is well worth driving to for
the splendid panoramic view out over the village and its
vineyards. A few kilometres east of Laudun on the D9 is a
large, beautifully maintained medieval castle known as
Château de Lascours (*see* hotels), complete with moat and
corner towers. It was added to in the 17th and 18th
centuries, and today functions as a hotel.

From Laudun, take the D121 north to Orsan, a small
village surrounded by vines. Like St-Victor-la-Coste,
Orsan falls under a larger Villages *commune* – Chusclan, in
this case, which is about two and a half kilometres away to
the northeast. Thus, even though the village possesses its
own *cave coopérative*, it is Chusclan's name that is printed
on the labels of all the Côtes du Rhône-Villages wine
produced here. Orsan's sights are few: the Neo-
Romanesque village church is relatively young by Rhône
standards (it dates from 1863), and of its modest castle, the
most striking feature is a square, narrow tower.

Leave Orsan via the D138 (crossing the N580 en route) and head for Chusclan, which is surrounded by an unexpected stretch of lush, green countryside – a legacy of the River Cèze, which runs right past the village. Like Laudun, Chusclan was one of the first four villages allowed by the decree of 1953 to use its name on its wine; like Laudun, too, its winemaking history stretches back to Roman times. As if to emphasise the importance wine plays in this community, the route into the village passes right by the local cooperative, which is surprisingly modern and makes practically all the local wine. In Chusclan, rosé is the speciality and is made in a fresh, vigorous style designed to be drunk young – many put it on a par with the best rosés of Tavel and Lirac – but its soft reds and lively white wines also deserve attention.

The centre of this community lies across the Cèze, on the north bank of the river, and its origins go back to the Bronze Age. Following the Roman occupation, it was the establishment of a Benedictine priory that assured Chusclan's status as a winemaking village. At the time, white wine was the order of the day, and records indicate that dessert styles were being made as well. In the 16th century, the Counts of Grignan owned a respected vineyard in the area, and in 1629, King Louis XIII was offered four casks of white wine made from it when he visited nearby Pont-St-Esprit. By 1750, wine from Chusclan was being exported to England, the Low Countries and elsewhere; in 1812, it was the most expensive in the whole Gard *département*. The 20th century, however, has seen its fortunes ebb and flow, mainly following the fashion for or against rosé. Modern Chusclan remains a small, quiet village with a few narrow streets that cluster around the local church.

In contrast, Bagnols-sur-Cèze (to the east, along the N580) is a large dormitory town with about 18,000 inhabitants. Although there is a local cooperative and a few

Laudun (above, left) and Chusclan (above) are two of the first four villages allowed to use their names on local wines in addition to the usual 'Côtes du Rhône' title. In both villages, too, winemaking dates back to Roman times.

Château de Montcaud
Bagnols-sur-Cèze
Tel: 4 66 89 60 60
Urban bustle seems far away here, but this very comfortable hotel with 30 rooms is just a few kilometres west of Bagnols on the D6. The rooms are stylish and large. There is a park, swimming pool and tennis court. The restaurant is the best in Bagnols and its cellar is amply stocked with wines of the region.

St-Jean-Baptiste
Pont-St-Esprit
Tel: 4 66 39 33 24
Situated on the south side of town, on the N86, and surrounded by a park, St-Jean-Baptiste has nearly 30 rooms, all decorated with thought and care. Swimming pool, but no restaurant; however, the friendly proprietress cooks evening meals if they are booked in advance.

Valaurie
St-Nazaire
Tel: 4 66 8 66 22
A quiet, modern hotel set among pine trees and offering about 20 classically furnished rooms. St-Nazaire is on the N86, near Vénéjan. No restaurant, but in summer, grilled dishes can be prepared for guests.

domaines base their offices here, water seems more important to this community than wine. Bagnol's name comes from the Latin *bagneola*, meaning 'little bath', because there were sulphurous baths in the town during Roman times. Consequently, you will find three baths displayed on the town's coat of arms.

The rectangular Place Mallet, surrounded by arcades, forms the heart of Bagnols, and the 14th-century Tour de l'Horloge, built by Philip the Fair, stands near it. The 17th-century *hôtel de ville* (town hall) is also situated by the square, and it houses Bagnols' *Musée de Peinture* (Museum of Painting). It is well worth a visit, for it contains works by such 19th- and 20th-century artists as Albert Marquet (*Le 14 juillet au Havre*, 1906), Renoir (*Jeunes femmes la campagne*, 1916) and Matisse (*La fenêtre ouverte*, 1919). West of Place Mallet is the Rue Albert Andréruns, where you can admire the town's oldest house, number 12, which dates from the 13th-century. Bagnols-sur-Cèze also has a *Musée d'Archéologie* at number 24 Rue Paul Langeon, where artefacts dating from the Iron Age and the Gallo-Roman period are on display.

From Bagnols, head north on the N86, then turn left onto the D980 and drive west to the wine village of St-Gervais. Although small and unassuming, St-Gervais was granted its own Côtes du Rhône-Villages AC in 1974, as is testified by the vineyards which run down the surrounding hills towards the river. Mostly Grenache and Cinsaut are planted and vinified into red and rosé wines in the local co-op, but a few private growers have been experimenting fairly successfully with white wines. One of the best producers of Villages wines, Domaine Ste-Anne, is established in the hamlet of Les Cellettes, three kilometres north of St-Gervais. The road runs uphill, offering a view of the clay and limestone soils – sometimes arranged in terraces – where the vines grow.

The little centre of St-Gervais, with its tiny stone houses and worryingly narrow streets, is full of atmosphere. Besides its charming *lavoir* (washhouse), it boasts a medieval church with two towers; inside is a broken column from a Roman monument, and by the south wall, part of a sarcophagus.

From St-Gervais, drive back to the N86, turn left, and then right on the D148 to Vénéjan, a pretty little Provençal village settled on the flanks of two hills. The Cave Coopérative de Vénéjan is considered to be one of the finest in the entire Côtes du Rhône appellation. Although it makes some rosé wine, its greatest talents are displayed in its reds, which are generally well-balanced with plenty of blackcurrant fruit.

On the more northerly of Vénéjan's two hills stands the magnificent Château des Ancézune, in private ownership and sadly not open to the public; on the hill to the south is the beautifully restored 12th-century chapel of St-Jean-Baptiste, from whence there is a beautiful view. Otherwise,

RESTAURANT

Les Compagnons
Laudun
Tel: 4 66 79 34 96
This restaurant is established in an 18th-century building beside the church. Strictly regional cooking is offered, such as *cassoulet au confit d'oie*, and fresh fish dishes.

LOCAL ATTRACTIONS

● The *Camp de César*, up on a plateau, can be reached via Orsan. There you will see remains of fortifications of various periods, including a Roman tower.
● From Chusclan, you can walk to the impressive ruins of the 13th-century Gicon castle.
● Wednesday is market day in Bagnols-sur-Cèze.
● *Foires la Brocante* (antiques and flea markets) are usually arranged at Bagnols-sur-Cèze for the third Saturday in the month and on a Sunday at the end of June.
● First Sunday in July: antiques and flea market at Pont-St-Esprit.
● Saturday is market day in Pont-St-Esprit.

the steep, narrow cobblestone streets at Vénéjan support a cluster of stone houses, some of which are covered in wisteria blossom in the spring.

Above The Provençal village of Vénéjan, spread across two hills, is said to have one of the best coopératives in the Côtes du Rhône appellation.

From Vénéjan, follow the winding GR 42 north to Pont-St-Esprit. Along the way, wine-lovers could make a detour west to St-Alexandre; as a village, it is not remarkable, but it is home to a couple of good wine producers.

A small town with a population of about 8,500, Pont-St-Esprit forms the meeting point for three regions: the Languedoc, Provence and the Rhône-Alps. The town took its present name from its bridge, which was completed in 1309 with 25 arches of varying sizes, and is still used a great deal. For about seven centuries, this was one of just three bridges across the Rhône; the others were at Lyon and Avignon.

On the riverside quay south of the bridge, two churches dominate the Pont-St-Esprit skyline. The larger of the two is St-Pierre, a former monastery church built in the 18th century. Beside it stands the (mostly) medieval St-Saturnin, now a parish church with a belltower from a later date. From the quay, climb the broad, monumental steps that lead up to the church of St-Pierre and the adjacent Place St-Pierre, where there is a good view of the Rhône and the bridge. It is just a short walk from the Place St-Pierre to the Place de l'Ancienne Mairie, where the *Musée Paul Raymond* is located. Its diverse displays include an extensive range of earthenware, china and apothecary's jars, as well as paintings, religious art and archaeological finds.

Pont-St-Esprit is where our journey through the west bank villages of the Côtes du Rhône ends. The final route leads eastward back across the Rhône to the separate appellations of Gigondas, Vacqueyras and the Côtes du Ventoux, with a stop at the fortified wine region of Muscat de Beaumes-de-Venise along the way.

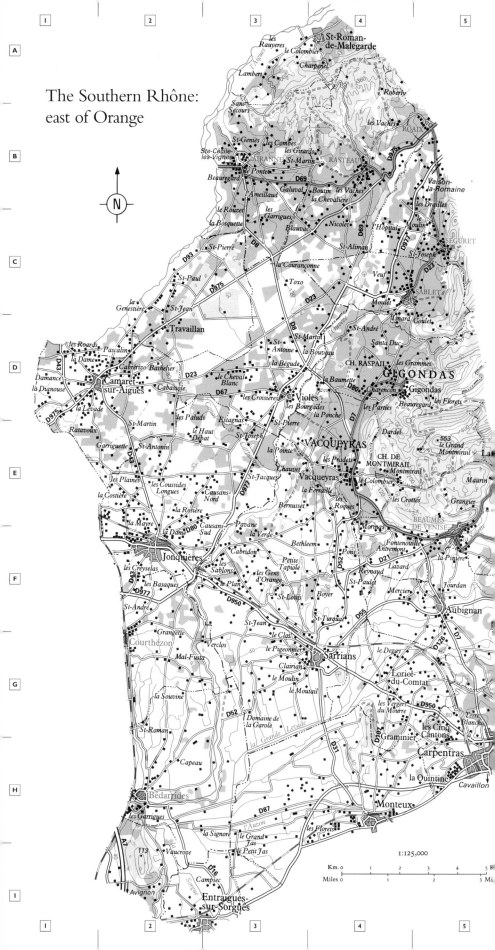

The Southern Rhône: east of Orange

GIGONDAS

A minuscule hamlet, not far from Mont Ventoux, and nestled at the foot of the hills which eventually stretch themselves into the jagged, limestone peaks of the Dentelles de Montmirail mountain range... no one can say that Gigondas is impressive due to its size. With about 700 inhabitants, it is hard to believe that the village has lent its name to one of the southern Rhône's three great red-wine appellations.

Approximately 90 per cent of wine bearing the Gigondas name is red (the rest is rosé derived from *saignée de cuve*, or bleeding off red grape juice). It is one of the strongest reds produced in the entire Rhône Valley, which reflects the high percentage of Grenache (up to 80 per cent) used in its blend; Syrah and Mourvèdre (either separately or together) account for the remainder. Once used as a 'booster' wine to improve weak Burgundy in much the same way as Hermitage was used to bolster Bordeaux, Gigondas won its own AC in 1971 – a victory for the local *vignerons*, who had been working for years to raise standards. Today, Gigondas is a deep, almost black-red wine, powerful and earthy but with a great depth of brambly, raspberry fruit and a long life-expectancy. In the wrong hands, it can prove heavy and lack finesse, but top estates turn out a wine that is an excellent partner for game, spicy dishes and strong-flavoured cheeses.

All of which makes it even more surprising that, right up until the mid-20th century, olive groves dominated the landscape around Gigondas. It was not until two devastating frosts – the last one in the 1950s – threatened to destroy the villagers' livelihoods that most of them began growing vines on a larger scale. Even so, the first vines were planted in the region by Roman centurions who had country villas here, and the name Gigondas stems from the Latin *Jocunditas*, meaning 'Happy Town' – a reference, perhaps, to the effects of the local wine.

Above *Appearances are deceptive in Gigondas. In this sleepy little village, over 30 private estates, a couple of* négociant *firms and a* coopérative *all bottle and sell wine.*

_.._.._ Département boundary

_..._.._ Arrondissement boundary

_..:._.._ Canton boundary

.._....... Commune (parish) boundary

CH. DE
MONTMIRAIL Leading producer

Bédarrides Châteauneuf-du-Pape commune

SABLET Côtes du Rhône-Villages commune

_____ Appellation communale boundary

▢ Vineyards

▢ Woods

Contour intervals:
below 120 metres every 20 metres
above 120 metres every 40 metres

▬▬ Wine route

GIGONDAS

RECOMMENDED PRODUCERS

Domaine la Bouissière
Try the Cuvée La Font de Tonin.

Domaine du Cayron
Top-class wines are made by this estate.

Clos du Joncuas
Fernand Chastan makes wines which are powerful, complex and harmonious.

Domaine Font-Sane
One of the few estates in this region to have a woman winemaker.

Domaine les Goubert
Jean-Pierre Cartier makes worthy Gigondas, aged in new wood.

Domaine du Gour de Chaule
This family-run estate produces round, supple wines.

Domaine de la Grapillon d'Or
Bernard Chauvet turns out fine, rich Gigondas, some from 80-year-old vines.

Domaine les Pallières
The Roux family has run this estate since the 15th century.

Domaine de Piaugier
The *domaine* produces supple wines with plenty of tannin for ageing.

Château Raspail
One of the most celebrated estates in the Rhône, run by Christian Meffre.

Domaine Raspail-Ay
Makes elegant wines with the minimum of chemical interference.

Domaine St-Gayan
This reputable estate produces reliable Gigondas from old vines.

Domaine de Santa Duc
Produces powerful, firm wines.

Domaine les Teysonnières
The wines at this estate are generous yet tough enough to last.

Domaine la Tourade
The estate also makes Vacqueyras alongside reliable Gigondas.

Domaine les Tourelles
Produces full, balanced wines with a remarkable texture.

Les Vignerons de Gigondas
The co-op offers a range of good wines, including the Cuvée du Président.

Pierre Amadieu
The largest vineyard owner here, making substantial, firm wines.

HOTEL
Les Florets
Tel: 4 90 65 85 01
Set in a peaceful location 2km from the village, Les Florets offers 13 very comfortable rooms. The restaurant serves good country cooking and a good selection of local wines.

Right *Vineyards flourish where once olive trees dominated the landscape. Viticulture did not take off around Gigondas until the 1950s.*

During the Middle Ages, viticulture flourished thanks to the bishops of Orange, who, after being replaced by the Avignon popes, spent more time at the nearby abbey of St-André to the northwest, where the nuns had been growing both vines and olives for years. Winemaking at Gigondas continued steadily but uneventfully throughout the centuries, until the aforementioned frosts. Today, an estimated 650 people out of the total of 700 depend on winemaking for a living.

You can sample a good cross-section of Gigondas at the local Caveau du Gigondas, run by the Syndicat des Vins, where around 40 growers store their wines. The Caveau is located in the Place de la Mairie, the main square in the village, which is shaded by plane trees. Tasting and sales premises of individual producers, the *office de tourisme* and a restaurant may also be found on the Place. Even higher up in the village (and, thankfully, accessible by car) stands the church of Ste-Catherine, which dates from the 11th century and has an open belfry. The interior has gilded wooden figures ascribed to Jacques Bernus (*see* Côtes du Ventoux, page 138). Beside the church are the ruins of a castle, where volunteers are busy restoring its walls. The view from up there is beautiful, and in clear weather you can see the Cevennes. High above Gigondas, on the north side of the village, is a narrow road that leads past various wine estates to the hotel-restaurant Les Florets, a peaceful, secluded hostelry set in the midst of pine trees. On a slope beside the road is the little chapel of St-Cosme, which was partly destroyed during the religious wars, but later restored. Like almost everything else in Gigondas, its name has been incorporated into the local industry – in the form of the Domaine St-Cosme wine estate.

VACQUEYRAS

The distance between Gigondas and Vacqueyras is short – about three kilometres – and the Dentelles du Montmirail remain as a backdrop as you travel south from Gigondas along the D7. Otherwise, the two villages have little in common. For a start, Vacqueyras is one of the newest Rhône appellations, having been promoted to its own AC status from Côtes du Rhône-Villages in 1990. In 1994, it had about half the area under vine that neighbouring Gigondas had, and those vineyards tended – and still tend – to contain a higher percentage of Cinsaut, although Grenache remains the dominant variety.

Like Gigondas, however, red wine is the most commonly produced in Vacqueyras (the AC does allow some white wine production), and it comes with a firm structure. As well as their alcohol and tannin, the best Vacqueyras reds possess a pleasant measure of fruit, a pinch of spice and a certain refinement and character sometimes lacking in heftier Gigondas wines.

Vacqueyras itself is built on a hillside at some distance from the Dentelles. It has had a relatively unremarkable history, apart from being the home of a talented medieval troubadour called Raimbaud who had a brief but illustrious life. (The local co-op is called 'Le Troubadour' in his honour.) On the top of the hill, sections of wall and two gates are all that remain of the castle which stood here in the Middle Ages, but one of its great underground halls now functions as the local wine-tasting centre. A painting in the neighbouring church commemorates the darker side of winemaking: on April 11, 1767, all the vines around

Above Vacqueyras has had its own appellation for just a few years, but its wine often shows a certain finesse.

RESTAURANT
l'Oustalet
Tel: 4 90 65 85 30
Stop here for strictly traditional cuisine. l'Oustalet is situated in a fine house in the Place de la Mairie.

VACQUEYRAS

RECOMMENDED PRODUCERS
Domaine des Amouriers
Produces firmly structured wines of excellent quality.
Arnoux & Fils
Uses the name Vieux Clocher.
Cave des Vignerons
Le Troubadour
Also vinifies wines from the estates, such as those from Château des Hautes Ribes. The Cuvée des Vieilles Vignes comes from 50-year-old vines.
Domaine du Clos de Caveau
The estate is counted among the leading growers of Vacqueyras.
Domaine Clos des Cazaux
The Archimbaud-Vache family runs things here, making Gigondas from mountain vineyards and Vacqueyras from old vines.
Domaine le Couroulou
Makes good, reliable wines.
Domaine de la Fourmone
Produces balanced, reliable wines.

Domaine de la Garrigue
Try the Cuvée Vignoble Vacqueyras prestige. Also makes Gigondas.

Domaine des Lambertins
The estate uses carbonic maceration to make some of its wines.

Domaine de la Monardière
A very dependable estate.

Château de Montmirail
An important estate. The cellars are on the right as you drive into the old centre of the village. Belongs to the Archimbaud family.

Domaine des Montvac
Can be relied upon for good Vacqueyras.

Pascal Frères
Wine firm on the border of Vacqueyras and Gigondas, which has links with a Burgundian concern, and also runs an excellent Gigondas estate. The wines are of a good average quality.

Château des Roques
Considered to be among the best domaines in Vacqueyras.

Domaine des Tours
Here you can find well-made wines of good quality, outside the village along the D950.

WINE FAIRS AND FESTIVALS

● On and around July 14: Vacqueyras celebrates a large wine festival.

 HOTELS

Hôtel Montmirail
Tel: 4 90 65 84 01
Located a few kilometres outside the village, towards the mountains, this is a rustic place, with somewhat old-fashioned, rather dark rooms that are nevertheless very comfortable. There is also a park and a swimming pool, and a regional-style restaurant.

Le Pradet
Tel: 4 90 65 81 00
Built in 1990, Le Pradet features 20 fairly small, tastefully decorated rooms. Although situated near quite a busy road, it is quiet inside, partly because of the thick walls. The bathrooms look almost Scandinavian. No restaurant.

RESTAURANT

Les Dentelles
Tel: 4 90 65 86 21
Situated on a street corner by the main road, Les Dentelles offers honest regional cooking at reasonable prices.

Vacqueyras were destroyed by frost, reducing the growers of the time to despair. Perhaps they were able to wash away some of the depression in the old communal *lavoir* (washhouse), which is located in a lower section of the village near the Domaine des Lambertins cellar.

If the washhouse didn't do the trick, one could always go to the Station Thermale de Montmirail, a spa situated one and a half kilometres east of Vacqueyras. It attracted some 1,000 guests a year, including such celebrities as Sarah Bernhardt and Frédéric Mistral. Besides the hot springs, the complex boasted a hotel and casino, the remains of which can still be seen.

BEAUMES-DE-VENISE

From Vacqueyras, continue heading south along the D7 to the village of Beaumes-de-Venise. Along the way, just before the turning onto the D81, you will pass the chapel of Notre-Dame-d'Aubune, a Romanesque jewel of a building. The main structure dates from the ninth or tenth century, while the square tower with its unglazed windows is from a slightly later period. It is thought that the chapel marks the site of an eighth-century victory by the Gauls over the invading Saracens. The losers were forced to hide in the caves and grottoes that riddle the surrounding hills – hence the name of the village, for 'Beaumes' comes from a Provençal word for 'grotto'. Vines grow in front of the chapel, and behind it rises the same steep, grey wall of rock that, further on, shelters Beaumes-de-Venise itself from the north winds.

Not only does Beaumes-de-Venise belong to the Côtes du Rhône-Villages AC, it also produces a luxurious, fortified, sweet white wine. This is called Muscat de Beaumes-de-Venise, and it is easily the most widely known of France's *vins doux naturels*. The Muscat wine grapes which go into it are the only ones grown in the Rhône, and their natural sweetness is preserved by adding some alcohol during the fermentation process, which leaves unfermented sugar in the wine. As a result, Muscat de Beaumes-de-Venise possesses a honey-like, very fruity aroma (apricots, peaches, grapes) and a rich, grapey palate which, thankfully, isn't

Right   Lavender blooms near Beaumes-de-Venise, but here its vinous neighbours are most likely to be Muscat.

cloying. It makes a splendid partner for fresh fruit as well as for all kinds of desserts, but in recent years, the fashion has been to serve it as a chilled *apéritif*. Its beautiful golden colour, heady perfume and long, luxurious taste make it an essential part of a complete cellar for those who like the style; others may find it a somewhat overwhelming experience. The Cave des Vignerons, situated on the D7 and overlooked by the chapel of Notre-Dame d'Aubune, offers Muscat de Beaumes-de-Venise for sale alongside red, white and rosé Côtes du Rhône wines and wines from the Côtes du Ventoux.

The village of Beaumes-de-Venise is centred around a small square. Just as in the rest of the Rhône, winemaking here stretches back to Roman times, but the village has other items of interest from different periods in history. Close to the square, for example, stands the church of St-Pierre which possesses a *chasuble* – the outer vestment worn by a priest when celebrating mass – that was presented to the church by Queen Anne of Austria, mother of Louis XIV. There is also a small archaeological museum in the village, where exhibits include items taken from a prehistoric burial, in part of a system of underground caves known as the Cabanes d'Ambrosi.

From Beaumes-de-Venise, it is well worth driving seven and a half kilometres north on the D90 to Suzette for a truly marvellous view of the Dentelles de Montmirail. And from Suzette, it is but a short drive southeast to the village of Le Barroux, where our journey through the Côtes du Ventoux begins.

BEAUMES-DE-VENISE

RECOMMENDED PRODUCERS

Cave Coopérative Intercommunale des Vins et Muscats
A dynamic concern that is by far the biggest producer of Muscat de Beaumes-de-Venise, and has been unsparing in its efforts to make this dessert wine known in France and beyond. The wine is of good quality. This co-op also produces other wines, including Côtes du Rhône-Villages.

Domaine de Beaumalric
Situated across the bridge in the village, in the direction of Caromb.

Domaine Castaud-Maurin
Formerly Domaine des Bernardins.

Domaine de Coyeux
Makes exceptionally reliable Muscat de Beaumes-de-Venise. Yves Nativelle is the owner.

Domaine Durban
One of the most renowned producers in Beaumes.

Domaine de Fenouillet
A small estate, turning out good wines.

SUZETTE
Château Redortier
Large private producer of Muscat de Beaumes-de-Venise (two kinds, an ordinary and a Cuvée Spéciale). The vineyard extends around the site where the princes of Orange had a castle. The estate also supplies Gigondas and Côtes du Rhône-Villages.

WINE FAIRS AND FESTIVALS
● Beginning of July: Beaumes-de-Venise celebrates the *Fête du Muscat*.

RESTAURANTS
Auberge St-Roch
Tel: 4 90 62 94 29
Traditional regional dishes are served in the small, neat dining room. The Auberge also offers a few simple hotel rooms.

Les Relais des Dentelles
Tel: 4 90 62 95 27
Located opposite the previous restaurant. Here, too, you can eat good, affordable food – for example, *entrecôte à la crème de moutarde*. Also has hotel rooms (offering somewhat limited comfort).

Left *The chapel of Notre-Dame d'Aubune, which stands isolated in the landscape outside Beaumes-de-Venise.*

RECOMMENDED PRODUCERS

AUBIGNAN
Domaine St-Sauveur
This estate makes Muscat de
Beaumes-de-Venise in addition
to other wines.

BEDOIN
Les Vignerons du Mont Ventoux
The co-op produces good rosé
and white wines.

CAROMB
Cave St-Marc
This co-op makes good reds
full of fruit and spice.
It also houses a museum of old
agricultural implements.
Domaine Chaumard
The estate produces good wines
with balanced acidity.
Augustin Ribas
A leading grower in the Côtes
du Ventoux.

FLASSAN
Paul Coutelen
Coutelen has a reputation for
producing reliable wines.

MAZAN
Château la Croix des Pins
The Avon family runs this estate.
Domaine de Fondrèche
Fondrèche produces elegant wines
full of character.
Les Vignerons de Canteperdrix
Co-op producing balanced, quite
harmonious wines – despite the fact
that one of the label names is
Marquis de Sade.

MORMOIRON
Domaine des Anges
Malcolm Swan, from Britain and a
former advertising man, nowadays
produces a range of red wines which
are among the very best in the area.
Try his Clos de la Tour.
**Cave Coopérative
Les Roches Blanches**
Among its wines, the co-op produces
a 100% Syrah that is well worth trying.
Château Pesquié
Dynamically managed wine estate
that produces attractive red wines,
including a *cuvée prestige* made
from 40-year-old vines and
matured in cask.

THE COTES DU VENTOUX

To the east of Gigondas, Vacqueyras and the villages of the Côtes du Rhône lies the Côtes du Ventoux *appellation contrôlée*, a relative newcomer in many respects, since it achieved AC status only in 1973. Here, the wines are light and fresh, with a juiciness that makes them a natural choice on many of the region's restaurant and café tables. They are mainly red, and are made from the usual Rhône grape varieties – Grenache, Carignan, Cinsaut, Syrah and Mourvèdre, but they grow at a much higher altitude than in other Rhône appellations. In addition to the usual light reds, firm and even wood-aged Côtes du Ventoux are produced alongside some juicy rosés and a little white wine (though the latter is nothing special). The vineyard area here is extensive, since the appellation is made up of 51 *communes*; the most important of them lie in the gigantic natural amphitheatre formed by Mont Ventoux and its neighbouring peaks.

'The giant of Provence' is another name that is given to Mont Ventoux, the highest point in this part of southeastern France. At 1,909 metres high, the bare, rocky peak is covered in snow for much of the year. The road up to it is about 20 kilometres long, with gradients varying from one in 25 to one in seven – a nightmare for riders in the Tour de France, who have had to struggle

*Right The monastery at
Le Barroux. The village itself is a
delight, unspoiled by tourist traffic.*

over it at various times. The outline of Mont Ventoux, which is more massif than mountain, can be seen from many kilometres away and is a landmark for anyone visiting the southern Rhône Valley. The summit itself is rugged and unapproachable, but around its flanks stretches a beautiful landscape full of fruit trees, cypresses and olives – and, of course, the vineyards of the Côtes du Ventoux wine district.

Begin your journey through the Côtes du Ventoux in Beaumes-de-Venise. Just outside the village, you will be treated to a fine view of winegrowing country and of Mont Ventoux; there are many more such panoramas to come. From Beaumes-de-Venise, take the D21, then turn right on the D938 and drive on to Le Barroux.

Le Barroux is a delightfully un-touristy village which is perched on a rocky height that dominates the pass to Malaucène, further north – which is exactly why a fortified tower was built here during the 12th century. Four hundred years later, the *seigneurs* of Baux created a Renaissance château around it. This imposing structure, now a study centre for history and archaeology, has a terrace which overlooks the roofs of Le Barroux, with their round, Provençal tiles. Using the car up here is practically impossible, so park on the way into the village and discover the place on foot.

VILLES-SUR-AUZON
Cave Coopérative de Montagne Rouge
Another reliable co-op making sound Côtes du Ventoux.

WINE MARKET
● Fridays from mid-July to mid-August: wine market in Carpentras.

HOTELS

Le Beffroi
Caromb
Tel: 4 90 62 45 63
Le Beffroi is a simple country hotel with 8 rooms. It also features a restaurant.

Le Fiacre
153 Rue Vigne
Carpentras
Tel: 4 90 63 03 15
Twenty pleasant rooms are centred around a courtyard at the Fiacre, which is located in the old centre close to the *office de tourisme*. No restaurant, however.

Les Géraniums
Le Barroux
Tel: 4 90 62 41 08
The hotel is situated in an old stone building, high up and close to the centre of town; consequently, the view is very pleasant, and there are two terraces. Choose from 20 modernised, comfortable rooms. The restaurant serves generous helpings of the region's seasonal dishes, such as grilled lamb or game.

Hostellerie de Crillon-le-Brave
Crillon-le-Brave
Tel: 4 90 65 61 61
Tastefully furnished hotel located near the church, in the upper end of the village. There are 24 rooms in addition to a car park, swimming pool, garden and tennis court. The restaurant serves typical Provençal fare. This is the most comfortable place to stay along the route.

Safari Hôtel
1 Avenue Jean-Henri Fabre
Carpentras
Tel: 4 90 63 35 35
Situated away from the busy centre, on the Avignon road, the Safari is a modern complex of around 40 rooms and suites offering sumptuous comforts. It is surrounded by a park, and also has a swimming pool and a tennis court. Provençal specialities are served in the restaurant. There is no quieter place to stay in Carpentras.

Above *Thanks to a modern bypass, the village of Caromb has been allowed to retain most of its Provençal atmosphere.*

RESTAURANTS

La Mirande
Caromb
Tel: 4 90 62 40 31
This is a genial sort of place located by the church square and serving regional cuisine. It also offers a few simple hotel rooms.

l'Oustau d'Anaïs
Bédoin
Tel: 4 90 65 67 43
Good country food is available at this restaurant, which sits at the foot of Mont Ventoux. A convivial, relaxed atmosphere adds to its charms.

Le Vert Galant
12 Rue de Clapies
Carpentras
Tel: 4 90 67 15 50
Situated in a little street behind the church of Notre-Dame-de-l'Observance, the Vert Galant serves fine, inventive dishes based on ingredients fresh from the market. It's the best restaurant in the place, so you will need to book.

From Le Barroux, retrace part of your route by heading south on the D938, then turning left onto the D13, which leads to the village of Caromb.

Caromb is a typical Provençal village, with a couple of squares and fountains, plane trees and an atmospheric old centre that used to be fortified and is now (thankfully) bypassed. Aside from the simple pleasure of strolling through its streets, Caromb's other attractions include Notre-Dame des Grâces St-Maurice, a Gothic-style church topped by an octagonal tower that was built in the 14th and 15th centuries. Just outside the village is the local wine cooperative, the Cave St-Marc. It also houses the interesting *Musée des Vieux Outils* (literally, the 'Museum of Old Implements'), which displays agricultural tools from earlier centuries.

A narrow road runs east from Caromb to the tiny hamlet of Crillon-le-Brave, which gets its name from Berton de Balbe, a companion of Henri IV, who was nicknamed 'the brave Crillon' – though just why is unclear. His virtues must have been significant, however, at least enough to merit the statue of him which stands opposite the *mairie* (town hall) and an epitaph in the local medieval church which states: 'Henri IV loved him, the poor mourned him'. Besides its tributes to Berton de Balde, Crillon-le-Brave also possesses the remains of a 15th-century castle and parts of its 16th-century walls.

From Crillon, take the D138 east towards Bédoin, the next destination, a largish village of ochre-coloured houses which cluster together at the foot of Mont Ventoux. Bédoin is fairly tourist-orientated, as is clear from the many cafés and shops which line the shady, slightly sloping main street. This is not necessarily a bad thing, however, as local businesses include the Cave Coopérative des Coteaux du Mont Ventoux, which offers (among its other wines) some light, refreshing rosés for sale. Not everything over the years has come up roses in Bédoin, though; elsewhere in the village, a small obelisk commemorates a sad episode that occurred just after the French Revolution. On May 2,

1794, after a tree planted by the Revolutionaries was uprooted, 63 villagers were executed in retaliation – an action which makes the presence of the white Jesuit church seem rather ineffectual.

From Bédoin, follow the D974 west towards the hamlet of Les Baux. En route, you will see some strangely formed, pointed rock formations standing among the trees. They have been dubbed *Les demoiselles coiffées*, by the locals, a phrase which means 'the coiffured young ladies' – though the resemblance is not always immediately apparent.

From Les Baux, head south until you come to the D19, which leads into the village of Flassan. Just as in Bédoin, many of the houses here are built of the ochre-coloured stone which is quarried around Mont Ventoux. As well as yielding stone for the houses, the mountain also provides water for the many fountains scattered about the village.

Continue your journey south for about four kilometres on the D19 to Villes-sur-Auzon. This charming old village is home to a local wine co-op, the Cave Coopérative de Montagne Rouge. It also hosts a carnival every year, which begins on Ash Wednesday and lasts around four days.

Travel east now from Villes-sur-Auzon along the D942, turn right after about five kilometres, and follow signs into the village of Mormoiron. Stone quarrying and winemaking are two of the main businesses here, as can be seen from neighbouring quarries, vineyards and the local wine co-op. The streets are quite narrow and sometimes partly roofed over, and above the houses rises the imposing Church of the Annunciation, which was enlarged during the 18th century; its gilded altarpiece was made by Jacques Bernus (*see* Mazan below). Mormoiron also offers two museums for interested visitors. In the upper part of the village, the *Musée Archéologique et Paléontologique* exhibits finds from the distant past, while at the lower end, the *Maison des Pays du Ventoux* (the House of the Country of Ventoux) is devoted to the history of the local region.

From Mormoiron, head west to Mazan via the small back road which leads past the church of Notre-Dame de Pareloup. Mazan was originally built along this road, around

LOCAL ATTRACTIONS

● June: cherry festival in Caromb.
● There is a Tuesday market all year round in Mormoiron, plus one on Sunday mornings from April to December.
● May: Mormoiron organises an asparagus fair; a crafts fair is held at the same time.
● Friday is market day in Carpentras.

Below *Though larger than most villages in the vicinity, Bédoin is easily dwarfed by the splendour of Mont Ventoux.*

Top *The cosmopolitan atmosphere of Carpentras, with its museums, restaurants and shops, contrasts strongly with the more rural southern Rhône villages such as Aubignan* (above).

which dozens of sarcophagi have been found; 66 of them have been brought together in a lane beside the churchyard. The 12th- to 15th-century church itself was built partly underground to offer protection against packs of wolves. At roughly the same time (and probably partly for the same reason), defensive walls were constructed around Mazan itself; today, only a few of the gates remain. On a low hill in the centre of the village stands another old church – this time of medieval origin, although it was rebuilt several times – which displays works by the local artist, Jacques Bernus (1650-1728). In his day, Bernus was the most famous painter and sculptor in the region, and his works include the statue of St Roch in the local votive chapel.

Near the church are the remains of the Château de Sade, where Jean-Baptiste François, father of the notorious marquis, was born in 1702. The presence of this château explains why the local co-op uses the name 'Marquis de Sade' for one of its wines. The chapel of the Pénitents Blancs is also situated near the church and houses the small *Musée Municipal Historique et Folklorique* (the Museum of History and Folklore) underneath its painted roof.

From Mazan, it is just seven kilometres west (on the D942) to Carpentras. The bustle of Carpentras with the usual urban problems of beggars and unsavoury characters, contrasts strongly with the rural character of the other villages of the Côtes du Ventoux, but that is only to be expected from a busy city of around 30,000 people.

The city centre covers a rough rectangle, with the Place Charles de Gaulle at its heart. On the Place stands the large Palais de Justice, a former episcopal palace built by a 17th-century cardinal of Carpentras. Apparently, the cardinal was as worldly as his palace, for he commissioned Nicolas Mignard to decorate the walls with erotic frescoes of satyrs and nymphs; today's sightseers won't be able to view them, however, for they were covered over by one of his more pious successors. A Roman arch stands behind the Palais, which is attached on its south side to the 15th-century cathedral of St-Siffrein. A hundred years later, Jews entered the cathedral in chains, passing through the *Porte Juive*, or Jews' Gateway, to be symbolically freed into new lives as Christians. Works of art in the cathedral include some gilded statuary in the chancery – again, by Jacques Bernus.

Just south of the central area, near the Place Aristide-Briand, stands the enormous Hôtel-Dieu, an 18th-century building that is still used as a hospital. It is more interesting than most, however, because it has retained its original pharmacy. Here visitors can see displays of past remedies, which included cat's-foot extract and something purporting to be dragon's blood.

As befits a city of this size, Carpentras has several museums, among them the *Musée de la Poésie* (The Poetry Museum, on the Route de Pernes), founded in 1976. On the Boulevard Albert-Durand, the *Musée Duplessis* displays work by the local painter Joseph-Siffrein de Duplessis. In the same building you will find the city's *Bibliothèque Inguimbertine* (The Inguimbertine Library), while the northern part of the complex is devoted to the *Musée Comtadin*, the local history museum, where displays include a collection of sheep's bells with different pitches. North of the centre along the Rue d'Orange stands the only surviving relic of the medieval town walls, the huge, 14th-century Porte-d'Orange.

If you happen to be in Carpentras on a Friday, then be sure to take advantage of the weekly markets which stretch across the city, with stalls selling everything from pot plants to bric-à-brac. From November 27, on the Place du 24 Août 1944, the market includes truffles, while in April, strawberries are the order of the day.

From Carpentras, head southwest along the D942. This busy main road leads into Avignon, the city of the popes, where our tour through the Rhône Valley ends.

Below The village of Mazan is home to the ruins of Château de Sade, where the father of the notorious marquis was born.

Bristol
44 Cours Jean Jaurès
Tel: 4 90 82 21 21
This well-maintained hotel offers 60
rooms along one of Avignon's main
streets. No restaurant, though.

Cloître St-Louis
20 Rue du Portail Rouge
Tel: 4 90 27 55 55
This hotel was once a Jesuit cloister.
Today, it houses 80 rooms, a
swimming pool and a restaurant.

Le Médiéval
15 Rue Petite-Saunerie
Tel: 4 90 86 11 06
A 17th-century building featuring
around 30 rooms decorated in an
old-fashioned style, with prices which
– for Avignon – are fairly reasonable.

*Below The great city of the popes.
In Avignon, their legacy lives on in
the enormous Palais des Papes, which
clearly dominates the Old Town.*

AVIGNON

Mention Avignon, and some people will think of popes. More, however, are likely to think of one of the world's most famous bridges, the so-called Pont d'Avignon, which is still celebrated musically in French classes around the globe. This medieval bridge is actually called the St-Bénézet, and for hundreds of years it was one of the few permanent links between the two banks of the Rhône. Today, it stretches only halfway across the river from the city's northwest corner, since just four of the original 22 arches remain. The bridge has been in this condition since the 17th century, when the constant restoration needed to counter the ravages of the Rhône was given up as a lost cause. Besides innumerable dancing tourists, the Pont d'Avignon supports the Romanesque and Gothic chapel of St-Nicolas.

But what of the town to which the bridge led? While its history certainly did not begin with them, Avignon – together with many of its monuments and churches – is inextricably tied to the medieval papacy. It was in 1309 that Pope Clement V moved the official papal residence here to avoid troubled times in Rome – a 'temporary' measure that lasted for seven decades and had a profound effect upon the

city and its people. For a start, it resulted in the construction, in various stages, of what is now called the *Palais des Papes* – the Palace of the Popes. As expected, the *Palais* is a monstrously large complex set on the Place du Palais, dominating the *Vielle Ville*, or Old Town of Avignon. This is where seven Avignon popes resided during the 14th century – as well as two antipopes after the Great Schism of 1377 – and just how powerful these spiritual leaders were is apparent from the sheer scale of this immense, fortified Gothic residence with its 50-metre-high towers.

In fact, the Palais consists of two structures which surround a large courtyard. Visitors can view the *Palais-Nouveau*, or New Palace, which was built by Clement VI, who also managed to buy Avignon from the queen of Naples and Provence. Among the rooms open to the public are audience chambers and Clement's bedroom and study which, due to their lavish murals of fishing, hunting and other courtly and very worldly pursuits, reveal a good deal about their owner.

The *Palais-Vieux*, or Old Palace, was commissioned by Clement's predecessor, Benedict XII (pope: 1334–1342), and reflects his more austere and paranoid attitudes to life –

RESTAURANTS

Christian Etienne
10 Rue de Mons
Tel: 4 90 86 16 50
One of the best restaurants in Avignon, situated near the south side of the papal palace in a 12th-century building. The menu offers fine, regional cuisine and a splendid choice of wines.

Les Domaines
28 Place de l'Horloge
Tel: 4 90 82 58 86
This wine bar has a large terrace and serves conscientiously prepared regional cuisine.

Le Grangousier
17 Rue Galante
Tel: 4 90 82 96 60
Provençal cooking receives an original twist at this excellent restaurant within walking distance of the papal palace.

Below *Avignon's hôtel de ville is situated on the Place de l'Horloge, which forms a welcome oasis of cafés for weary tourists seeking refreshment.*

Above *The Pont St-Bénézet, otherwise known as the Pont d'Avignon, famed in French classes throughout the world.*

not so much by design, however, as by default, for fire and the ravages of time have left little of the original decoration and furnishings intact. The tour of the Old Palace begins in the Salle de Consistoire, where the pope conferred with his cardinals and received important visitors. Next to this room, the chapel of St-Jean has fine frescoes by Matteo Giovanetti. These and the many other rooms are now largely empty, but it is not difficult to imagine how grand it must all have been when the popes held court here and the whole place was lavishly furnished. Fantastic costly banquets were arranged for visiting monarchs and dignitaries, and if the walls could talk, many visitors would be dismayed at the stories they could tell of intrigue, adultery, corruption and worse that went on inside them. Not for nothing did the 14th-century Italian poet Petrarch call Avignon 'a sewer where all the filth of the universe has gathered', for in the wake of the popes came a flotilla of merchants, doctors and lawyers, heretics on the run from Rome, clerks, criminals and con men. It gave truth to the medieval maxim that 'city air makes a man free' – mainly because, in this case, one could disappear into anonymity and (literally) get away with murder.

Where there is corruption, it has to be paid for – hence, across the square from the Palace stands the *Hôtel des Monnaies* (the Mint) with a richly decorated façade. The *Petit-Palais*, on the north side of the same square, was where papal guests – monarchs and princes among them – were lodged; today it houses a huge collection of medieval painting and sculpture. Immediately north of the Palace is the cathedral of Notre-Dame-des-Doms, which dates from the 12th century, but was later rebuilt and enlarged; consequently, the interior has been 'Baroqued' to the extreme. The fine tower has also been embellished with a gigantic statue of the Virgin Mary. Among the notable items inside are a marble throne; the tomb, in Flamboyant style, of Pope John XXII (to whom Châteauneuf-du-Pape owed its 'new castle'); and frescoes by Simone Martini. For a break from the buildings, visit the *Rocher des Doms*, a beautiful garden-like park north of the cathedral where you can relax on a bench and enjoy the view.

There are several museums in Avignon, and it is difficult to decide which ones to pursue, but the *Musée Calvet* at 65 Rue Joseph-Vernet definitely deserves a visit. It is an easy walk south of the Palace (about 600 metres away, west of the busy Rue de la République). The eclectic collection includes paintings of all periods by such masters as Géricault, Brueghel and Dufy, sculpture by Rodin, Egyptian mummies, Gallo-Roman pottery and some splendid wrought-iron work. An annexe, in a former chapel, houses the *Musée Lapidaire* (the Lapidary Museum), which displays mainly Gallo-Roman archaeological finds.

All of which barely scrapes the surface of historic Avignon, but don't forget: there is a living city here, too. After sightseeing in the papal quarter, you might head southwest to the busy Place de l'Horloge for a glass of wine at one of the many cafés. Or you could lose yourself in the many tangled streets of the Quartier de la Banasterie, east of the Place du Palais, where there are also plenty of cafés and restaurants to help you on your way again. For information on wine, you could pay a visit to the *Maison du Vin* at 6 Rue des Trois Faucons, which provides details on wines from throughout the entire Rhône Valley.

But considering that you have just completed this journey through the Rhône's wine regions yourself, I very much doubt that you will need it.

Below *The fresh produce of Avignon's markets ends up in its restaurants' quality cuisine – the perfect partner for Rhône wines.*

GLOSSARY

Apéritif – an alcoholic drink imbibed before a meal to stimulate the appetite. The word has its root in the Latin *aperire*, 'to open', which is what it is meant to do to the digestive system

Appellation (d'Origine) Contrôlée (AC or AOC) – regulations which provide strict control of origin, alcoholic strength, quantity produced, grape varieties and methods used in French wine production. The exact nature of the AC varies from region to region, but the model for them all stems from the Rhône Valley, based on the legislation drawn up by the association of French *vignerons* led by Baron Pierre Le Roy de Boiseaumarie (see pages 18 and 19)

Autoroute – the term used for a main motorway in France; most are *autoroutes à péage*, or toll roads

Barrique – a barrel. In Bordeaux and Cognac, it refers specifically to an oak barrel holding 225 litres (or 300 bottles) of wine

Bibliothèque – library

Bureau/office de tourisme – tourist information office

Cave – can be used to refer to a cellar or to most any wine establishment

Cave coopérative – a cooperative winery run by and for wine-growers

Chailée – narrow terrace used for growing vines in the northern Rhône

Chambres d'hôte – literally, 'rooms of the host': rooms let to tourists by private citizens, similar to a B&B in the UK

Charcuterie – pork butcher's shop and delicatessen; also refers to the cooked pork meats and pork offal products themselves

Château – while the word literally means a castle or large house, in wine terms it refers to any wine estate, regardless of size

Chêne truffiers – truffle oaks: the specific type of oak trees under which truffles grow

Commune – refers either to a town or village, or to the area that surrounds the town or village – i.e. a district or parish

Côte – literally means 'hillside', but in wine terms it refers generally to a particular vineyard that is considered far superior to vineyards on surrounding plains. When used in names of *appellations contrôlées* (Côte-Rôtie, etc) it means the same thing

Coteaux – means the same as *côte* (see above)

Cuvée – refers to wine contained in a *cuve*, or vat. In certain wine regions – e.g. Champagne – the term is synonymous with 'first pressing'; elsewhere it is used simply to refer to 'blend'. Often, though, it merely refers to one 'lot' or 'batch' of wine, and can be used to mean a bottled wine

Dauphin – historically, the eldest son of the king of France

Département – a territorial division which refers to one of the 95 main administrative divisions or regions of France

Domaine – similar in meaning to *château*, but more usually refers to the property or estate, not the 'house' itself

Doré – literally means 'gilt' or 'golden', but in wine terms, refers to the 'bronze' or brown type of Rasteau *vin doux naturel*

Doux – literally, 'sweet'. *See vin doux naturel*

Entrecôte – rib steak. *Côtes* in this instance means 'ribs'; hence a piece of prime quality beef which should be cut from 'between the ribs'

Formule rapide – literally, 'rapid formula'; a quick set menu

Galets – literally, 'pebbles'. In wine terms, these are large, roundish stones found in vineyards of the southern Rhône (especially in Châteauneuf-du-Pape) which act as natural storage heaters, reflecting the sun's warmth to the grapes and hastening and concentrating the ripening process

Hectare (ha) – a measure of area, usually considered to be 2.47 acres

Hôtel de ville – town hall

Jeu de boules – the game of bowls

Langoustine – a marine crustacean that resembles a crayfish, e.g. scampi

Lavoir – washhouse; usually communal stone structures found in older Provençal villages

Macération carbonique – French term for carbonic maceration. A fermentation process used in making red wines in which fermentation takes place without the intervention of yeasts or even crushing the grapes. Whole bunches of grapes are put in a closed vat filled with carbon dioxide. Each grape ferments internally, a process which eventually explodes the grapes and yields mild, fruity wine designed for drinking young

Magret – a portion of meat taken from the breast of a duck that has traditionally been fattened for *foie gras*

Mairie – another term for town hall

Maison du vin – 'house of wine'; usually a wine merchant or small shop offering wine for sale

Marc – grape-skins left over after pressing. Also the strong-smelling brandy that is produced from them, similar to Italian Grappa

Marché aux Vins – a wine market or (sometimes) wine fair

Méthode dioise ancestrale – sparkling winemaking process used in the production of Clairette de Die. In it, base wines are fermented in stainless-steel tanks for very low temperatures, then the wine is filtered and bottled. Fermentation continues in bottle until the wine reaches an alcoholic strength of 7.5% alcohol by volume, and the wine is disgorged six to 12 months later, filtered again, and put in new bottles

Méthode champenoise – French term for the sparkling winemaking process used in the production of champagne. The use of this term has been banned in the EU since 1994, and has now been replaced by either *méthode traditionnelle* and *méthode traditionnelle classique*.
It is the most labour-intensive and meticulous method of making sparkling wine, and involves refermenting the wine in its bottle

Mistral – the cold, northerly wind that blows down the Rhône Valley and southern France before heading out into the Mediterranean. Although it produces headaches among many people subjected to it, it also helps to keep vineyards disease free

Miel – honey

Morille – morel; a rare mushroom that grows only in spring

Musée – museum

Négociant – a merchant or shipper (can be an individual person or a firm) who buys wine in bulk or bottle to sell under own labels

Nougat – a sweet made from sugar, honey and nuts. It has its roots in a Roman sweetmeat called *nucatum* (from the Latin nux, meaning 'nut'), but the modern version seems to have originated in Marseille, where it used walnuts as its base. In Montélimar, almond-based nougat became the norm; the almond content in Montélimar nougat is usually 30%

Palais – palace

Pétanque – a type of bowls played in the South of France

Picodon – a goats-milk cheese with a fat content of 45%, a soft centre and a natural crust that is blue, golden or red, depending upon the ripeness.

The name comes from a Languedoc word *pico*, meaning 'to sting', and the cheese has a strong or highly nutty flavour

Pont – bridge

Pontias – a soft, late-afternoon breeze that blows in and around the city of Nyons, adding to the unique microclimate that gives the city its nickname of 'little Nice'

Poulet fermier– a free-range chicken

Rancio – term for the desired nutty tang found in brown, wood-aged *vin doux naturel* and other fortified wines. In table wines, it is considered a fault

Saigner (saignée de cuve) – Bleeding off the juice from a vat of red grapes. The practice is used particularly in dilute vintages in order to concentrate the remaining juice

Sandre – pike-perch

Sentier viticole – literally, a 'wine' or 'wine-growing path'; usually a footpath or trail which has been set up in and around vineyards

Tapenade – a Provençal condiment made from capers, desalted anchovies and stoned black olives, all of which are pounded together in a mortar and seasoned with olive oil and lemon juice. It accompanies crudités or can be spread on slices of toast

Tarte aux fruits – fruit tart

Terroir – a problematic term that has no precise cognate in English. In general, it refers to the general physical environment of a vineyard, including the soil and all its layers, how it relates and reacts to the local climate and microclimate and how it ultimately influences the wine. Thus a wine from a specific vineyard will exhibit influences of *terroir* that are unique to that vineyard

Tian – an ovenproof earthenware dish used in Provence to create *gratin* dishes of the same name

Tour – tower

Tranquille – French term for still or non-sparkling wine

Trufficulteur – a truffle-grower

Typicité – a wine-tasting term (the English equivalent is *typicality*) which refers to a wine's quality being typical of its style, geographic location or even vintage. The term is used mainly by professional wine tasters, who cannot always agree on what it consists of when it pertains to individual wine styles; therefore, it is entirely subjective

Vendange – harvest

Vigneron – wine-grower

Vignoble – an area of vineyards

Vin de pays – freely translated, 'country wine'. The term as a category came into use in 1973, and refers to from specific origins, such as a particular village or an entire region or département, such as *Vin de Pays du Gard*. There are more than 140 *vin de pays* names currently in use, and they fall into three categories: regional, departmental and something called *Vin de Pays de Zone*, which is the most precise classification

Vin doux naturel – sweet wine that has been fortified with wine alcohol, which arrests the fermentation process and leaves some of the 'natural sweetness' of the grapes in the finished wine

Vinum picatum – Latin term for wine fortified with pitch; in Roman times, pitch was the only 'preservative' available that would allow wine to travel without spoiling

Viticulteur – a wine-grower

GAZETTEER

INDEX

PICTURE CREDITS

Front and back Jacket: Michael Busselle

Les Belles Image/Erik Spaans 26/7, 65. **Michael Busselle** 5 centre bottom, 12 /13 bottom, 42, 51, 53 bottom, 72, 92, 130, 132. **Hubrecht Duijker** 44 /45, 56 top left, 66 /67, 69, 73, 74, 118, 123, 124, 125, 127. **Robert Harding Picture Library/Roy Rainford** 113. **Hendrik Holler/Root Stock** 5 top, 6, 8 /9, 12 /13 top, 16 /17 bottom, 18 /19 bottom, 20, 22 /23, 35, 39, 43 bottom, 54, 58 /59, 62, 63, 114 /115 bottom, 117. **Image Bank /Pascal Perret** 84. **Scope /Philippe Blondel** 78/79, **/Chris Cheadle** 24 bottom, **/Jacques Guillard** 3, 5 bottom, 5 centre top, 9 top, 12 bottom, 14 top, 14 /15 bottom right, 16 bottom, 18 /19 top, 21, 22 bottom, 24 /25 top, 28 /29, 29 top, 30, 31, 32, 33, 36, 38, 40 /41, 43 top, 45 top, 46, 47, 48 /49, 50, 52, 53 top, 55, 56 /57 top, 59 top, 60/1, 64, 68, 70 /71, 75, 76, 77, 78 top, 80, 81, 85, 86, 87, 88, 89, 90, 91, 93, 94, 95, 96, 98, 99, 100, 101, 102, 103, 104, 105, 107, 108, 109, 111, 112, 115 top, 116, 119, 120, 121, 122, 129, 131, 133, 134 /135, 136, 137, 138 bottom, 138 top, 139, 140, 141, **/Michel Guillard** 37, **/Noel Hautemanière** 142, 143, **/Georges Simon** 14 /15 bottom, 106